Praise for *The Brethren*

"Explosive. . . . The most controversial book on the Supreme Court yet written."

—*Los Angeles Times Book Review*

"Fascinating. The pace is swift, with details that rivet the attention."

—*The Washington Post Book World*

"A provocative book about a hallowed institution. . . . It is the most comprehensive inside story ever written of the most important court in the world. For this reason alone it is required reading."

—*BusinessWeek*

"It is to the credit of Woodward and Armstrong that they were willing—and able—to shatter this conspiracy of silence. It is certainly in the highest tradition of investigative journalism."

—*Saturday Review*

"One hell of a reporting achievement."

—*The Village Voice*

"The year's best political book."

—*New York Post*

Also by Bob Woodward

Rage

Fear: Trump in the White House

The Last of the President's Men

The Price of Politics

Obama's Wars

The War Within: A Secret White House History, 2006–2008

State of Denial

The Secret Man (with a Reporter's Assessment by Carl Bernstein)

Plan of Attack

Bush at War

Maestro: Greenspan's Fed and the American Boom

Shadow: Five Presidents and the Legacy of Watergate

The Choice

The Agenda: Inside the Clinton White House

The Commanders Veil: The Secret Wars of the CIA, 1981–1987

Wired: The Short Life and Fast Times of John Belushi

The Brethren (with Scott Armstrong)

The Final Days (with Carl Bernstein)

All the President's Men (with Carl Bernstein)

Also by Scott Armstrong

Chronology (with Malcolm Byrne and Tom Blanton)

The Brethren (with Bob Woodward)

THE JUSTICES BEHIND
ROE V. WADE

THE INSIDE STORY

Adapted from *The Brethren*

BOB WOODWARD

AND

SCOTT ARMSTRONG

Simon & Schuster

NEW YORK   LONDON   TORONTO
SYDNEY   NEW DELHI

Simon & Schuster
1230 Avenue of the Americas
New York, NY 10020

First Simon & Schuster trade paperback edition October 2021

SIMON & SCHUSTER and colophon are registered trademarks
of Simon & Schuster, Inc.

For information about special discounts for bulk purchases,
please contact Simon & Schuster Special Sales at 1-866-506-1949
or business@simonandschuster.com.

The Simon & Schuster Speakers Bureau can bring authors to your
live event. For more information or to book an event, contact the
Simon & Schuster Speakers Bureau at 1-866-248-3049
or visit our website at www.simonspeakers.com.

Interior design by Paul Dippolito

Manufactured in the United States of America

1   3   5   7   9   10   8   6   4   2

Library of Congress Cataloging-in-Publication Data is available.

ISBN 978-1-9821-8663-0
ISBN 978-1-9821-9608-0 (ebook)

To Katharine Graham, Chairman of the Board,
The Washington Post Company,
for her unwavering commitment to an independent press
and the First Amendment.

And to our children, Tali, Thane and Tracey

A court which is final and unreviewable needs more careful scrutiny than any other. Unreviewable power is the most likely to self-indulge itself and the least likely to engage in dispassionate self-analysis. . . . In a country like ours, no public institution, or the people who operate it, can be above public debate.

Warren E. Burger, Circuit Court of Appeals Judge, to Ohio
Judicial Conference on September 4, 1968—nine months
before being named Chief Justice of the United States

CONTENTS

AUTHORS' NOTE

Two people labored as long and as hard on this book as the authors.

Al Kamen, a former reporter for the *Rocky Mountain News*, assisted us in the reporting, writing and editing of this book. He was the chief negotiator and buffer between us. His thoroughness, skepticism and sense of fairness contributed immeasurably. No person has ever offered us as much intelligence, endurance, tact, patience and friendship.

Benjamin Weiser, now a reporter for *The Washington Post*, helped in the research, writing, editing and reporting. A devoted and resourceful assistant, no one could have been more loyal and trusted.

This book is as much theirs as ours.

INTRODUCTION

THE UNITED STATES SUPREME COURT, THE HIGHEST court in the land, is the final forum for appeal in the American judiciary. The Court has interpreted the Constitution and has decided the country's preeminent legal disputes for nearly two centuries. Virtually every issue of significance in American society eventually arrives at the Supreme Court. Its decisions ultimately affect the rights and freedom of every citizen—poor, rich, Black people, Indian people, pregnant women, those accused of crime, those on death row, newspaper publishers, pornographers, environmentalists, businessmen, baseball players, prisoners and presidents.

For those nearly 200 years, the Court has made its decisions in absolute secrecy, handing down its judgments in formal written opinions. The Court's deliberative process—its internal debates, the tentative positions taken by the justices, the preliminary votes, the various drafts of written opinions, the negotiations, confrontations and compromises—is hidden from public view.

The Court has developed certain traditions and rules, largely unwritten, that are designed to preserve the secrecy of its deliberations. The few previous attempts to describe the Court's internal workings—biographies of particular justices or histories of individual cases—have been published years, often decades, after the events, or have reflected the viewpoints of only a few justices.

Much of the history, notably the period that included the continued court-ordered desegregation of public schools, the Vietnam War, and the role of the states in regulating abortion, suggests that the detailed steps of decision making, the often hidden motives of the decision makers, can be as important as the eventual decisions themselves. Yet the Court, unlike the Congress and the presidency, has by and large escaped public scrutiny. And because its members are not subject to periodic reelection, but are appointed for life, the Court is less disposed to allow its decision making to become public. Little is usually known about the justices when they are appointed, and after taking office they limit their public exposure to the Court's published opinions and occasional, largely ceremonial, appearances.

The Justices Behind Roe v. Wade is an account of the inner workings of the Supreme Court from 1969 to 1973—the first four years of Warren E. Burger's tenure as chief justice of the United States. However, it is not intended as a comprehensive review of all the important decisions made during the period.

The Court conducts its business during an annual session called a *term*, which begins each October and continues until the last opinion is announced in June or early July. The Court recess runs from then until the next October.

Normally, there are seven decision-making steps in each case the Court takes.

1. The decision to take the case requires that the Court note its jurisdiction or formally *grant cert*. Under the Court's procedures, the

justices have discretion in selecting which cases they will consider. At least four of the nine justices must vote to hear a case. These votes are cast in a secret conference attended only by the justices, and the actual vote is ordinarily not disclosed.

2. Once the Court agrees to hear a case, it is scheduled for *written and oral argument* by the lawyers for the opposing sides. The written arguments, called legal briefs, are filed with the Court and are available to the public. The oral arguments are presented to the justices publicly in the courtroom; a half hour is usually allotted to each side.

3. A few days after oral arguments, the justices discuss the case at a closed meeting called the *case conference*. There is a preliminary discussion and an initial vote is taken. Like all appellate courts, the Supreme Court normally uses the facts already developed from testimony and information presented to the lower trial court. The Supreme Court can reinterpret the laws, the U.S. Constitution and prior cases. On this basis, the decisions of lower courts are affirmed or reversed. As in the cert conference, at which justices decide which cases to hear, only the justices attend the case conferences. (The nine members of the Court often refer to themselves collectively as the conference.)

4. The next crucial step is the selection of one of the nine justices to write a majority opinion. By tradition, the chief justice, if he is in the initial majority, can *assign* himself or another member of the majority to write the opinion. When he is not in the majority, the senior justice in the majority makes the assignment.

5. While one justice is writing the majority opinion, others may also be drafting a *dissent* or a separate *concurrence*. It can be months before these opinions—a majority, dissent or concurrence—are sent out or circulated to the other justices. In some cases, the majority opinion goes through dozens of drafts, as both the opinion and the reasoning may be changed to accommodate other members of a potential majority or to win over wavering justices. As the justices read the drafts, they may shift their votes from one opinion to another. On some occasions, what had initially appeared to be a majority vanishes and a dissenting opinion picks up enough votes to become the tentative majority opinion of the Court.

6. In the next to last stage, the justices *join* a majority or a dissenting opinion. Justices often view the timing, the sequence and the explanations offered for "joins" as crucial to their efforts to put together and hold a majority.

7. In announcing and publishing the final *opinion*, the justices choose how much of their reasoning to make public. Only the final versions of these opinions are available in law libraries. The published majority opinion provides the legal precedents which guide future decisions by lower courts and the Supreme Court itself.

We began this project in the summer of 1977 as two laymen lacking a comprehensive knowledge of the law. We read as many of the cases and as much of the background material about the period as time would allow. We found the work of Derrick Bell, Paul Brest, Lyle Denniston, Fred Graham, Eugene Gressman, Gerald Gunther, Richard Kluger, Nathan Lewin, Anthony

Lewis, John MacKenzie, Michael Meltsner, John Nowak, Ronald Rotunda, Nina Totenberg and Laurence Tribe particularly helpful. We thank them, and countless others on whose writings we have drawn.

Most of the information in this book is based on interviews with more than 200 people, including several justices, more than 170 former law clerks, and several dozen former employees of the Court. Chief Justice Warren E. Burger declined to assist us in any way. Virtually all the interviews were conducted "on background," meaning that the identity of the source will be kept confidential. This assurance of confidentiality to our sources was necessary to secure their cooperation.

The sources who helped us were persons of remarkable intelligence. They had unusually precise recall about the handling of cases that came before the Court, particularly the important ones. However, the core documentation for this book came from unpublished material that was made available to us by dozens of sources who had access to the documents. We obtained internal memoranda between justices, letters, notes taken at conference, case assignment sheets, diaries, unpublished drafts of opinions and, in several instances, drafts that were never circulated even to the other justices. By the time we had concluded our research, we had filled eight file drawers with thousands of pages of documents from the chambers of the 11 justices who served during the period 1969 to 1973.

For each of the four terms we describe, we had at least one, usually two, and often three or four reliable sources in each justice's chamber, in no case fewer than 20 sources per term. Where documents are quoted, we have had direct access to the originals or to copies. We have attributed thoughts, feelings, conclusions, predispositions and motivations to each of the justices. This information comes from the justices themselves, their diaries or memoranda, their statements to clerks or colleagues, or their positions as regularly enunciated in their published Court opinions. No characterization of a justice could be comprehensive, but we believe those that are provided help explain the decisions and actions.

Bob Woodward
Scott Armstrong

PROLOGUE

EARL WARREN, THE CHIEF JUSTICE OF THE UNITED States, hailed the elevator operator as if he were campaigning, stepped in and rode to the basement of the Supreme Court Building, where the Court limousine was waiting. Warren easily guided his bulky, 6-foot-1-inch, 220-pound frame into the backseat. Though he was 77, the chief still had great stamina and resilience.

Four young men got into the car with him that fine November Saturday in 1968. They were his clerks, recent law graduates, who for one year were his confidential assistants, ghostwriters, extra sons and intimates. They knew the "Warren Era" was about to end. As chief justice for 15 years, Warren had led a judicial revolution that reshaped many social and political relationships in America. The Warren Court had often plunged the country into bitter controversy as it decreed an end to publicly supported racial discrimination, banned prayer in the public schools, and extended constitutional guarantees to Black people, poor people, Communists, and those who were questioned, arrested or charged by the police. Warren's clerks revered him as a symbol, the spirit of much that had happened. The former crusading prosecutor, three-term governor of California, and Republican vice-presidential nominee had, as chief justice, a greater impact on the country than most presidents.

The clerks loved their jobs. The way things worked in the chief's chambers gave them tremendous influence. Warren told them how he wanted the cases to come out. But the legal research and the drafting of Court opinions—even those that had made Warren and his Court famous and infamous—were their domain. Warren was not an abstract thinker, nor was he a gifted scholar. He was more interested in the basic fairness of decisions than the legal rationales.

They headed west, downtown, turned into 16th Street and pulled into the circular driveway of the University Club, a private eating and athletic club next to the Soviet Embassy, four blocks north of the White House. The staff was expecting them. This was a Saturday ritual. Warren was comfortable here. His clerks were less so. They never asked him how he could belong to a club that had no Black members.

As Warren and his clerks moved to lunch, the chief expressed his frustration and his foreboding about a Nixon presidency. Earlier that year, before the election, Warren had tried to ensure a liberal successor by submitting his resignation to President Lyndon B. Johnson. The Senate had rejected Johnson's nominee, Associate Justice Abe Fortas, as a "crony" of the president. All that had been accomplished was that Nixon now had Warren's resignation on his desk, and he would name the next chief justice.

Warren was haunted by the prospect. Supreme Court appointments were unpredictable, of course. There was, he told his clerks, no telling what a president might do. He had never imagined that Dwight Eisenhower would pick him in 1953. Ike said he had chosen Warren for his "middle of the road philosophy."

Later Eisenhower remarked that the appointment was "the biggest damned-fool mistake I ever made."* Well, Warren said, Ike was no lawyer. The clerks smiled. But Richard Nixon was, and he had campaign promises to fulfill. He must have learned from Eisenhower's experience. He would choose a man with clearly defined views, an experienced judge who had been tested publicly on the issues. The president would look for a reliable, predictable man who was committed to Nixon's own philosophy.

"Who?" asked the clerks.

"Why don't we all write down on a piece of paper who we think the nominee will be?" Warren suggested with a grin.

One clerk tore a sheet of paper into five strips and they sealed their choices in an envelope to be opened after Nixon had named his man.

Warren bent slightly over the polished wooden table to conceal the name he wrote.

Warren E. Burger.

———

Three months later, on the morning of February 4, 1969, Warren Burger, 61, was in his spacious chambers on the fifth floor of the court of appeals on Pennsylvania Avenue, almost midway between the White House and the Supreme Court. President Nixon, who had been in office only two weeks, had invited him to swear in several high-ranking government officials at the White House. When he arrived at the mansion, Burger was instantly admitted at the gate.

---

* Congressional Quarterly's *The Supreme Court: Justice and the Law*, 2nd ed., p. 163.

Nixon and Burger first met at the Republican National Convention in 1948. Nixon was a freshman congressman and Burger was floor manager for his home-state candidate, Minnesota governor Harold Stassen. At the next convention, four years later, Burger played an important role in Eisenhower's nomination. He was named assistant attorney general in charge of the Claims Division in the Justice Department, and in 1956 he was appointed to the United States Court of Appeals for the District of Columbia.* On that famously liberal court, Burger became the vocal dissenter whose law-and-order opinions made the headlines. He was no bleeding heart or social activist, but a professional judge, a man of solid achievement.

Now at the White House, the ceremonial swearings-in lasted only a few minutes, but afterward the president invited Burger to the Oval Office. Nixon emphasized the fact that as head of the Executive Branch he was deeply concerned about the judiciary. There was a lot to be done.

Burger could not agree more, he told the president.

Nixon told him that in one of his campaign addresses he had used two points from a speech Burger had given in 1967 at Ripon

---

* There are three levels of courts in the federal judiciary:—District courts with about 600 judges; these judges, at the first step in the federal system, hear and try cases.—Circuit courts of appeal; there are 11 of these intermediate circuits numbered First (New England states) through Tenth (Western states) plus the Circuit for the District of Columbia. There are from 4 to 14 appeals court judges in each circuit. These judges hear appeals from the district courts and interpret the Constitution, Supreme Court rulings and federal laws.—The Supreme Court, with nine members, reviews decisions made by both federal courts and state courts and handles other matters, such as disputes between states.

College in Wisconsin. *U.S. News & World Report* had reprinted it under the title "What to Do About Crime in U.S." The men agreed that *U.S. News* was the country's best weekly newsmagazine, a Republican voice in an overwhelmingly liberal press. Burger had brought a copy of the article with him.

In his speech Burger had charged that criminal trials were too often long delayed and subsequently encumbered with too many appeals, retrials and other procedural protections for the accused that had been devised by the courts.

Burger had argued that 5-to-10-year delays in criminal trials undermined the public's confidence in the judicial system. Decent people felt anger, frustration and bitterness, while the criminal was encouraged to think that his free lawyer would somewhere find a technical loophole that would let him off. He had pointed to progressive countries like Holland, Denmark and Sweden, which had simpler and faster criminal justice systems. Their prisons were better and were directed more toward rehabilitation. The murder rate in Sweden was 4 percent of that in the United States. He had stressed that the United States system was presently tilted toward the criminal and needed to be corrected.

Richard Nixon was impressed. This was a voice of reason, of enlightened conservatism—firm, direct and fair. Judge Burger knew what he was talking about. The president questioned him in some detail. He found the answers solid, reflecting his own views, and supported with evidence. Burger had ideas about improving the efficiency of judges. By reducing the time wasted on routine administrative tasks and mediating minor pretrial wrangles among lawyers, a judge could focus on his real job of hearing cases. Burger also was obviously not a judge who focused only on individual cases. He was concerned about the system, the prosecutors, the accused, the victims of crime, the prisons, the effect of home, school, church and community in teaching young people discipline and respect.

The president was eager to appoint solid conservatives to federal judgeships throughout the country. As chairman of a prestigious American Bar Association committee, Burger had traveled around the country and must know many people who could qualify. The president wanted to appoint men of Burger's caliber to the federal bench, including the Supreme Court. Though the meeting was lasting longer than he had planned, the president buzzed for his White House counsel, John Ehrlichman.

Ehrlichman came down from his second-floor office in the West Wing. Nixon introduced them. "Judge Burger has brought with him an article that is excellent. Make sure that copies are circulated to others on the White House staff," Nixon said. He added that Burger had constructive, solid ideas on the judicial system as well as for their anticrime campaign. Judge Burger was a man who had done his homework. "Please make an appointment with him to talk," the president said, "and put into effect what he says." The chat had turned into a seventy-minute meeting.

Ehrlichman left, concluding that if ever a man was campaigning for elevation in the judiciary, it was Warren Burger. He was perfect, clearly politically astute, and he was pushing all the right buttons for the president. Burger and Ehrlichman never had their follow-up meeting, but from press accounts and bar association talk, Burger knew that Nixon had designated Attorney General John Mitchell, his former campaign manager and law partner, to help find him new judges, including a new chief justice.

Mitchell, Burger understood, was the "heavy hitter," the one closest to the president. Privately, Burger had expressed doubts to friends whether a New York bond lawyer had the experience to be the nation's top law-enforcement officer.

On February 18, Mitchell asked for Burger's help. Shortly thereafter, Burger called at his office in the Justice Department. Knowing that Burger had numerous contacts in legal and judicial circles, Mitchell sought recommendations for nominees to the federal bench. Burger offered some names, and Mitchell wrote down the suggestions. Richard Kleindienst, Mitchell's deputy, sat in on the end of the hour-long meeting. After Burger left, Mitchell remarked, "In my opinion there goes the next chief justice of the United States."

A month passed. On April 4, Burger wrote a letter to Mitchell on his personal stationery. "In one of our early conversations you asked me to give you my observations on district judges and others over the country who might warrant consideration for appointment or promotion," Burger said. He offered three immediate suggestions, adding that "each of these men is especially well qualified." One of the three names he sent was a federal district judge in Florida, G. Harrold Carswell. Burger also promised to send along other recommendations "from time to time." Mitchell responded with a thank-you note the same day. Later that month, Burger received an invitation to a White House dinner that the president would give on April 23 to honor Chief Justice Warren.

The president's toast to Warren was glowing, and Warren in turn rose to praise Nixon. He was concluding his 40 years of public service, he said, with "no malice in my heart."

The next day, Burger's longtime archenemy on the appeals court, liberal Chief Judge David L. Bazelon, approached him. Cordially, he pointed out that Burger was the only district or circuit judge at the dinner. "Looks like you're it," Bazelon said.

"No," Burger said, brushing off his old adversary. To Burger, the 59-year-old Bazelon was a meddler—the self-appointed protector of every racial minority, poor person and criminal defendant.

But Washington reporters had also picked up the possible significance of Burger's White House invitation and began asking him about it. Burger was humble. He neither knew nor expected anything. Asked about other candidates for chief justice whose names were making the rounds, such as Secretary of State William Rogers, Burger downgraded each one. "No, no," he would tell reporters confidentially, "he wouldn't be good." The media made Burger a dark-horse candidate, but there was still a front-runner—Associate Justice Potter Stewart.

———

A week later, the morning of Wednesday, April 30, Stewart arrived at the Supreme Court late. He hated starting early. Stewart had impressive academic and establishment credentials. Born into a distinguished and wealthy family of Ohio Republicans, he had studied at Hotchkiss and Yale University, where he was Phi Beta Kappa and the editor of the *Yale Daily News*, before enrolling at Yale Law School, where he was a top student. At age 39 he was appointed by Eisenhower to the Sixth Circuit Court of Appeals. "I can promise you he is not too old," a leading Senate supporter had said. Stewart quickly came to love the work. He remarked that it involved "all the fun of practicing law without the bother of clients." Four years later, in late 1958, Eisenhower elevated Stewart to the Supreme Court, one of the youngest justices in history. For a decade, he had dissented from most of the major Warren Court opinions. Now, at 54, he was at his prime, perhaps ready for the final step.

That morning Stewart went straight to his chambers, staring at the marble floor, by habit avoiding eye contact with those he met along the way. A shy man, Stewart was of average height and build, with thin brown hair combed straight back from a receding hairline. In the men's club atmosphere of the Court, Stewart had found a comfortable shelter. The job was nearly perfect, providing both the prominence of a high government post and intellectual satisfaction, without overexertion. Reaching his chambers, he called John Ehrlichman at the White House. Stewart said he wanted a brief appointment with the president.

Ehrlichman called back shortly. Would three o'clock be okay? He fished for a clue, saying that he had told the president only that it was some matter involving the Court. "Was that enough to tell him?"

Yes, that was enough, Stewart said. Now he was committed to meet with the president, but he still had several hours to think. Stewart knew that he had supporters from Ohio, the Middle West and in GOP circles, who were urging that he be made chief justice. But did he really want it? If he got the job, the new era would become "the Stewart Court." Technically, the chief was only first among equals, but the post of chief justice had definite prestige.

On the other hand, the chief's vote counted no more than that of any of the other eight justices. The chief also had the additional chores of administering the Court and managing the building. In terms of pure lawyering, it was better to be an associate justice. All law and no nonsense. Did he want to be involved in all the tedious little decisions? To oversee committees and groups like the Judicial Conference, which was a "board of directors" of the federal judiciary and the judges' lobby? No, he concluded, he did not want to be bothered. If he got the job of chief, he would rarely see his family and have even less time to relax. His summers at his Bowen Brook Farm in New Hampshire would be disrupted. On a superficial level, there were big pluses. On a deeper level, there were not so many. Less law. More bureaucracy.

There were other considerations. Stewart had seen what President Johnson's feeble attempt to get his friend Abe Fortas moved from associate to chief had done to the Court. There had been other troubled times when associates had been promoted. The process of getting confirmed might be both contentious and some fun, Stewart thought. A likely target for critics might be his 1964 opinion ruling that a French film, *The Lovers*, was not hardcore pornography *(Jacobellis v. Ohio)*. He could not define obscenity, he had written, but "I know it when I see it." It might not be the height of legal sophistication, but the remark expressed Stewart's Middle Western pragmatism.

The biggest adjustment would be a loss of privacy. Associate justices could live private and relatively anonymous lives. That would change. The job of chief was considered by some to be the most powerful position after the presidency. There would be another FBI check, a Senate investigation, and hearings before the Senate Judiciary Committee. The press would become more interested in him. And when he got down to it, that was perhaps the biggest problem. When he had been nominated for the Court in 1958, then Deputy Attorney General William Rogers had asked Stewart if there was anything in his past that might embarrass him or the administration. Stewart had thought of some things—an editorial he had written for the *Yale Daily News* endorsing Democrat Franklin D. Roosevelt for president in 1936; or perhaps that particularly drunken evening in his sophomore year.

But nothing serious. Now it was a little different. Was it fair to his family? Would he have to wonder whether his private business might appear in the newspapers, if only in a gossip column?

Stewart left his chambers in plenty of time to be at the White House before 3 p.m. His stomach knotted as he drove through the Washington traffic. He was being awfully presumptuous. The president had not offered him the job. But if he took himself out of the running, he wouldn't have to deal with temptation if it came. If the position were actually offered, it would be harder to say no. Stewart drove through the White House gates and was escorted into the Oval Office.

Nixon greeted him warmly.

The president talked about whom he might pick as his chief justice. "Potter," Nixon said, "there has been an awful lot of support for you."

Stewart said he knew that there had been speculation, the inevitable lists. But he had come, he said, to tell the president that he didn't want it, that he didn't want to be considered, that he wanted to be out of the running.

Stewart recited his speech. In his opinion there were inherent, perhaps insurmountable, problems in promoting one of the sitting justices. Historically it had not worked. The chief justice had a special role to play as leader of the Court and it might disturb relationships that had been worked out over the years to appoint one of the eight associates to be chief. Promoting a sitting justice would not be the best way, Stewart said.

Nixon paused. "Let me remember who is on the Court," he said. First he mentioned the hapless Fortas. Nixon looked at Stewart. Slowly he listed the others.

Fortas, Stewart thought? Was the president thinking of

appointing Fortas? No, absolutely not; out of the question. But Stewart realized it was possible that Nixon was thinking of another sitting member. The only other Republican was John Harlan, but he was almost seventy and nearly blind. Perhaps Nixon was thinking of a Democrat?

Stewart mentioned that Roosevelt had elevated Harlan Stone, a Republican, to chief justice on the eve of World War II as a nonpartisan act of national unity. Maybe that wouldn't be a bad idea, appointing a Democrat.

Nixon went down the list of Democrats. There was William Brennan, who had been appointed by Eisenhower, and there was Byron White . . . could Nixon be thinking of White? Unlikely. White had been a John F. Kennedy appointee, and Stewart knew what Nixon thought of the Kennedys.

Then Nixon mentioned Fortas again. Why? Stewart wondered. Why was Nixon bringing up Fortas? Did he want some reaction? Stewart had little to say about Fortas. It was obvious that it had been a mistake for Johnson to attempt the eleventh-hour elevation of his close friend and adviser. It had hurt the Court, had made for strange, uneasy relations among the members. Stewart said it would be better not to put the Court through that again, nominating someone from the ranks. But Stewart was a little uneasy. He mentioned his own position again and, in a general way, the needs and desires of his wife and children, their high regard for privacy. "It would be unfair to my family," he said.

Nixon said he understood. He asked more questions about the Court and its members. He was keenly interested, concerned about the federal courts. There was much to do, and as president he wanted to help.

Finally, the two men stood and shook hands, and Stewart left.

The meeting had taken longer than he had expected, but he felt a sense of relief.

As he drove back, Stewart regretted that he had given phony reasons for taking himself out, but it had been necessary to protect his family. It was odd the way the president kept bringing Fortas up. What was that about? Stewart wasn't sure he had done the right thing, but he felt better than he had felt in a long while.

————

Nixon was giving a good deal of thought to the Court. He wanted to make good on his campaign pledge to turn it around. Replacing Warren was not enough to break the back of the working Warren majority—which had included Warren himself; Fortas; Thurgood Marshall, the first Black member of the Court, who had been appointed by Lyndon Johnson; William J. Brennan, another Eisenhower appointee who had turned out differently than Ike had expected; and William O. Douglas, seventy, a radical libertarian famous for his controversial writings and life, both on and off the bench. Nixon snickered about Douglas's fourth wife, Cathy, who was 25 and a law student. "Some law firm will love to get her," he told Ehrlichman.

The five-man liberal majority had support on race and civil rights issues from Byron White and Hugo Black. A new conservative chief justice, with Stewart and Harlan, the only Republicans on the Court besides Warren, would still give the Court only three "strict constructionists"—those who opposed a sweeping, liberal interpretation of the Constitution. White and Black might join the conservatives in certain criminal cases, but one could never be sure. The president needed at least another seat to turn things around, and Douglas seemed most vulnerable to a quiet administration investigation. On taking office, Nixon lost no time putting various federal agencies to work on it. The Internal Revenue Service began an audit of Douglas's tax returns only five days after the president's inauguration. At the same time, the FBI was compiling information on Douglas's connections with Las Vegas casino owner Albert Parvin. Douglas was a director of the Albert Parvin Foundation. But the Douglas investigations were slow in bearing fruit.

Now, unexpectedly, another track opened up. John Mitchell's Justice Department was providing assistance to *Life* magazine in its attempt to establish that in 1966 Abe Fortas had accepted a $20,000 fee from a foundation funded by millionaire industrialist Louis Wolfson.* At that time Wolfson had been under investigation by the Securities and Exchange Commission, and had apparently bragged that his friend Fortas was going to use his influence to help. Wolfson was indicted and later convicted, and Fortas secretly returned the $20,000.

When Nixon was informed of the investigation, he realized that Fortas's actions were perhaps not necessarily criminal. But there was an opportunity not only to get Fortas off the Court but

---

* In a June 2, 1969, memo to Attorney General Mitchell, FBI director J. Edgar Hoover stated that a reliable source had informed the FBI that, "in connection with the investigation involving former Supreme Court Associate Justice Abe Fortas, the department furnished considerable information to William Lambert, writer for *Life* magazine, which not only enabled Lambert to expose the Fortas tie-in with the Wolfson Foundation but additionally kept Lambert advised regarding its own investigation into the matter. It is perhaps significant that Hoover did not name any individual, but simply "the Department of Justice." It suggests that his reliable sources indicated that the leaks were official, perhaps authorized by Mitchell.

to discredit his strident liberalism. The Fortas investigation became one of Mitchell's first action projects, and Nixon demanded almost minute-by-minute reports, personally calling the shots from the Oval Office.

On May 1, Mitchell received a memo from Assistant Attorney General William H. Rehnquist. If Fortas had helped Wolfson, it said, they could prosecute him. The next day, May 2, Ehrlichman received a single copy of the advance proofs of the *Life* article. Spread over six pages, it was headlined, "Fortas of the Supreme Court: A Question of Ethics." Mitchell had an aide call every major news organization in town to alert them. When the article was released on Sunday afternoon, May 4, Washington exploded. Republicans called for impeachment. Democrats and liberals were stunned.

But Nixon didn't want an impeachment. It would take too long and might in the end hurt the Court. All Nixon wanted was Fortas's seat, and he wanted it intact, not devalued. Resignation was the obvious shortcut. With the departure of Fortas and Warren, Nixon could name two justices. That would end the control of the liberals. In his first year, he would have altered the character of the Court.

On Tuesday, May 6, Wolfson surrendered to government investigators a document that showed that the $20,000 was not a one-time payment. The Wolfson Foundation had agreed to pay Fortas $20,000 a year for the rest of his life, or to his widow for as long as she lived.

When Mitchell arrived at Dulles Airport at 1:30 a.m. after a trip to New York, his aides showed him the documents. Mitchell was incredulous. He thought they might be phony. He was assured they were not. The news was forwarded to the president.

Nixon and Mitchell agreed that the attorney general should go to Earl Warren. With the Congress and editorial writers howling for Fortas's head, pressure from inside the Court might force the issue.

Entering the Court through the basement garage, Mitchell called on Warren in his chambers at 11:30 Wednesday morning. The meeting was to be confidential. Laying out the documents in his possession and referring to others, Mitchell outlined the developing case against Fortas. There was not only the contract specifying the annual payment, but he was about to obtain some Wolfson-Fortas correspondence in which the SEC case was discussed. In one letter Wolfson asked Fortas's help in obtaining a presidential pardon.

Warren thanked Mitchell and said that he appreciated the information. Mitchell mentioned how embarrassing this was for everyone. Approaching the subject delicately, he said that if Fortas were to resign voluntarily, the criminal investigation would "die of its own weight." An investigation would harm both Fortas and the Court more than a resignation would. Warren got the message.

From the beginning, Warren had been appalled at the disclosures about Fortas and had felt that Fortas must quit. The argument was now more compelling. After securing the support of several of the other justices, Warren launched a week-long campaign to get Fortas to resign. Only Douglas resisted overtly. He had been Fortas's professor and mentor at Yale Law School and later in Washington. Douglas himself had discussed retiring, but, loath to give Nixon a seat to fill, he decided not to retire while the Court was still under attack.

Nonetheless Douglas was surprised by Fortas's transgression. "God, how did Abe do such a stupid thing?" Douglas asked.

In Warren's view, Fortas had two problems that had led him to such indiscretion. As a private lawyer in Washington and a known intimate of the president, Fortas had made a fortune. He had had to take almost a 90 percent cut in salary when he came to the Court, and he had not wanted to alter his lifestyle.

Second, Warren concluded, as a bright man who had come to Washington during the New Deal, Fortas had made rules for others to follow, but had never thought they applied to him.

There were meetings and some heated sessions, and one week later, on Wednesday, May 14, Fortas sat down in his office and drafted his letter of resignation. He understood that all the evidence would be locked away. Jubilant, Nixon called Fortas to express his sympathy.

It was over for Fortas, but now two other Court liberals—Douglas and Brennan—came under attack for off-the-bench financial activities. Douglas was criticized for his $12,000-a-year directorship on the Albert Parvin Foundation. After 30 years on the Court, Douglas was accustomed to political attack. But the Fortas affair cast things in a different light. He decided to resign from the Foundation post on May 21.

Some conservatives went after the 63-year-old Brennan. News stories had raised questions about a $15,000 real estate investment he had with Fortas and some lower court judges, including Bazelon. Brennan was hurt by the criticism. He had grown up on the poor side of Newark and learned the rough-and-tumble of politics from his father, an Irish immigrant who was by turn a union leader, a Democratic politician and a police commissioner. After a brief tenure with a private law firm, Brennan served as a state trial, and then an appellate court, judge. In 1956, Eisenhower elevated him from the New Jersey State Supreme Court to the U.S. Supreme Court. Brennan's life was a model of upward mobility through conscientious public service. He was furious at the press for implying that his review of decisions by other judges would be influenced by the fact that they shared common investments. He suspected that the attack was led by those who resented his central role in the Warren Court, his unflagging support for unions and civil rights groups, and his votes restricting the powers of police.

In May, Brennan decided to lower his profile. "Well, guys," he said, walking into his clerks' office, "I'm eliminating all this." He formally canceled all future speaking plans, gave up his interest in the real-estate venture, sold his stock, quit his part-time summer teaching post at New York University, and even resigned from a board at Harvard University. He gave up every activity except the Court, his family and the Church.

One clerk who felt Brennan was overreacting asked him jokingly: "Did you write the pope?"

Brennan, the Court's only Catholic, was not amused.

The weekend after the Fortas resignation, Nixon was at Camp David, the presidential retreat in Maryland. With the liberals dazed by the Fortas revelations, it was time to choose his chief justice, perhaps the most important decision he would make as president. Mitchell had prepared a list of appeals court judges. Nixon wanted someone with judicial experience, someone whose views were fully predictable, not a crony or political friend, someone with integrity and administrative ability. Someone young enough to serve at least 10 years.

Warren E. Burger.

———

On May 19, the president instructed Mitchell to begin the necessary FBI investigation and report back at once. Burger checked

out. On Wednesday, May 21, Nixon told Mitchell to offer Burger
the appointment formally.

Only in Mitchell's office did Warren Burger learn that he
was to be named chief justice of the United States. He accepted
at once. A regular appointment to the Court would have been
enough. Chief was incredible. Already he felt a kinship with these
people, with Mitchell and Nixon. They were the men who had
taken over the national government, and they had selected him
over all others.

Nixon was obsessed with keeping the nomination secret until
he could announce it on national television that night. Burger
would be smuggled into the White House. Watching, Ehrlichman
thought Nixon seemed as interested in the secrecy as he was in
the appointment. Apparently Nixon felt that if he could make the
announcement before a leak occurred, he would have outwitted
the press.

Burger went home to prepare his family, making sure that
everyone looked proper for the ceremony. They were picked up
about 6 p.m., driven to the Treasury Department, and guided
down to the basement and through a long steam tunnel. They
made their way to the White House and came up in an elevator at
6:57, three minutes before airtime.

The president was waiting. He walked over to Burger.

As they stood chatting, Burger said: "Sometime when we have
more time to talk, I want to thank you for this."

At 7 p.m. Nixon and Burger walked before the cameras.
The next morning, the appointment was the lead story in every
newspaper. *New York Times* columnist James Reston wrote that
Burger was "experienced, industrious, middle-class, middle-aged,
middle-of-the-road, Middle-Western, Presbyterian, orderly, and

handsome." He took note of the liberals' and intellectuals' distress and added that "the old-boy network is grieving that the president did not elevate Associate Justice Stewart to the top job." *The New York Times* also quoted an unnamed judge who had worked with Burger on the court of appeals: "[Burger] is a very emotional guy, who somehow tends to make you take the opposition position on issues. To suggest that he can bring the Court together—as hopefully a chief justice should—is simply a dream."

Many who knew Burger's old foe, Bazelon, suspected that the comment was his. But Bazelon denied having talked to the press. "I was speechless and sick for a week," he said.

Burger stayed home to avoid the reporters who had gathered at the bottom of the driveway of his Arlington, Virginia, home. He requested that the reporters and cameramen be kept off the fifth floor at the court of appeals, where his office was, even though he was staying away. Later, he learned that the lobby had been filled with the press despite his request. "The only way they could have gotten in is Bazelon," Burger told his staff. "If I can prove it's true, I'll punch him in the nose."

———

Burger expected that his confirmation hearing before the Senate Judiciary Committee, which had to approve the nomination before it would be passed to the full Senate, might be a bloody battle. He envisioned a whole confederation of liberal interest groups planning to tear into him. "They're out to get me," he told his clerks as he brooded over the prospect. The opposition included Bazelon, the other liberals on the U.S. Court of Appeals for the District of Columbia, and some liberal justices like Brennan. It also included the young coat carriers, who seemed to rotate from a clerkship with Bazelon to a clerkship at the Court, perhaps for Brennan, before taking a job on the Hill, where they were always whispering into the ears of liberals like Senator Edward M. Kennedy at hearings.

Burger was sure that Kennedy would lead the opposition on the Senate Judiciary Committee. As a Republican nominee before a heavily Democratic Senate, he would be hard pressed. Nixon's pronouncements about changing the Court were an open challenge to the liberals.

Burger went to discuss the confirmation process with the chairman of the committee, Senator James O. Eastland of Mississippi. The aging conservative was a sure supporter. Eastland recommended that Burger use Eastland's own personal attorney, Roger Robb, already a close friend of Burger's, to assist him in the hearings. Burger took the advice. With Robb, he set up an office in the Watergate office complex, where they assembled records and previous opinions and tried to anticipate what curves the liberals might throw at Burger. They also gathered support from the organized bar associations, from law school deans, and from influential private attorneys.

Burger went to the Supreme Court one day and stopped by to see Brennan, the consensus builder in the Warren Court. Burger knew it was Brennan, with his instinct and passion for political maneuvering, who was the key strategist among the liberal bloc on the Warren Court. As Burger entered Brennan's chambers along the south corridor, he walked through the office used by Brennan's law clerks. There, hanging on a wall, was a grotesque rubber mask of Nixon, a souvenir of the counter inaugural demonstration that had been staged by antiwar activists and others opposed to the president. He recognized one of Brennan's clerks as a Bazelon clerk of the previous year. The clerk was scheduled to begin work for Kennedy on the Senate Judiciary Committee at the end of the term.

Learning that Brennan was not in the office, Burger turned to leave. On the inside of the door there was a Black Power poster with the clenched, raised fist. Burger sensed what he was up against. Brennan's law clerks did not share his values. They were part of a different world. Bazelon to Brennan to Kennedy.

———

On Tuesday, June 3, two weeks after his nomination, the Senate Judiciary Committee opened hearings. Burger was ready as the session opened at 10:35 a.m. Behind him in the audience sat six past presidents of the American Bar Association, 11 past presidents of the Federal Bar Association, and 12 past presidents of the District of Columbia Bar Association. All were prepared to speak in support of his nomination.

Burger was offered a few easy questions by Eastland and other members of the committee. Finally, from his hunched position, Eastland turned to the man Burger was certain would present him with a problem. "Senator Kennedy," Eastland mumbled.

"No questions, Mr. Chairman," Kennedy replied in his confident Boston accent.

Each senator took his turn, and there was not a word of criticism. The members seemed almost to compete with each other to praise Burger and take shots at the Warren Court. The hearing was adjourned in less than two hours and the committee unanimously recommended his confirmation to the Senate. Six days later the Senate voted 74 to 3 to confirm him. The process from nomination to confirmation had taken only 18 days.

A week later, only one week before he would be sworn in as chief justice, Burger was in his office at the court of appeals when he got some very distressing news. The Supreme Court had announced that it had overruled his court of appeals decision in a case involving the flamboyant New York Black congressman Adam Clayton Powell. The vote was an overwhelming 7 to 1, with Stewart the lone dissenter. Warren himself had written the majority opinion *(Powell v. McCormack)*. The press would have a field day.

The House of Representatives had voted to deny Powell his seat because he had flouted a slander judgment and allegedly had misused funds. Burger's opinion, one of three separate ones, held for the House against Powell. Powell had appealed to the Supreme Court, and now Warren had declared for a heavy majority that Congress could not deny the congressman his seat. The reversal was a typical example of the Warren Court's activism—mere meddling in Burger's view. He had already been overruled twice that year, but this was the first time since his nomination. There should have been some way for Warren to avoid a direct slap at him, perhaps with an unsigned opinion. Being reversed by the Supreme Court, however, would soon be a thing of the past. He could take comfort in that. In one more week, the Warren Era would be over.

Later that week, Burger left his office in the court of appeals and went out to Pennsylvania Avenue to meet Solicitor General Erwin N. Griswold, the man responsible for arguing the federal government's cases before the Supreme Court. Griswold had the presidential commission, signed by the president and the attorney general, that appointed Burger. It was to be delivered to the Court before the swearing-in.

Griswold and Burger took a cab to the Court, where Warren greeted them in his chambers. The Powell case was apparently on his mind. "I hated to decide for Powell," Warren told them.

Griswold thought Warren was going to explain the difficulty and awkwardness in overruling the next chief justice—perhaps apologize, saying that, of course, he had to call them as he saw them. Instead, Warren told them that he didn't like Powell and regretted having to decide in his favor. But as a matter of law, it would be impossible to let Congress exclude members in such fashion. In denying Powell his seat, Congress had asserted an absolute and unreviewable right to determine who was suited to sit, contrary to what the Constitution said. "It was perfectly clear," Warren remarked. "There was no other way to decide it. Anybody could see that."

My God, Griswold thought, Warren must not realize that Burger was one of the lower court judges he had just overruled. Griswold knew Warren did not write his own opinions, but was he so out of touch? The meeting was soon over and as they walked out, Burger good-naturedly shrugged off Warren's comment. "He certainly didn't give me much credit for what I did in the Adam Clayton Powell case," he told Griswold.

Burger had heard that Warren delegated the writing of his opinions to his clerks. That was only one of the many practices that he was going to stop. As far as he was concerned, the Warren legend was a fabrication. Burger used to talk scornfully to his clerks about Warren's liberalism. It was late in coming, he said. Warren had been aligned with the right wing of the Republican Party in California and was supposedly a states' rights champion. As governor he had strongly supported the internment of Japanese Americans during World War II. As district attorney, he had authorized offshore searches of questionable legality outside the three-mile limit. Burger told his clerks that Warren was "right-wing when it paid to be right-wing, then had shifted when that became fashionable."

On June 23, Burger joined the members of the Court, the president, Attorney General Mitchell, other ranking Justice Department officials, including FBI director J. Edgar Hoover, and members of the legal and Republican law-enforcement establishment for his swearing-in at the Supreme Court.

Since it was the last day of the term, the Warren Court first handed down its three final opinions. The decisions, all involving criminal cases, effectively overruled three more conservative precedents. They were precisely the kinds of opinions that Nixon had campaigned against.

Nixon, dressed in a formal cutaway, showed no emotion. When the last opinion was read, Warren recognized the president. Nixon stepped to the podium. "There is only one ordeal which is more challenging than a presidential press conference, and that is to appear before the Supreme Court." He reviewed Warren's career and praised the chief justice. But, he added, "The chief justice has established a record here in this Court which will be characterized in many ways."

In response, Warren gave a lecture—his last words from the bench—which seemed directed at Nixon. There was acid in the oblique graciousness. His theme was continuity. "I might point out to you, and you might not have looked into the matter, that it is a continuing body . . . the Court develops the eternal principles of our Constitution in accordance with the problems of the day." It was Warren's way of saying that Richard Nixon too would pass. The Court, Warren said, serves only "the public interest," is guided solely by the Constitution and the "conscience" of the individual justices. He was stepping down, Warren said, with a feeling of "deep friendship" for the other justices "in spite of the fact that we have disagreed on so many things.

"So I leave in a happy vein, Mr. President, and I wish my successor all the happiness and success in his years on the Court, which I hope will be many."

Part I

INTRODUCING THE JUSTICES

1969 TERM

BY JULY, CHIEF JUSTICE WARREN BURGER WAS IN his new offices. With three months before the start of the new term, and the other justices spending the recess at home or on vacation, he intended to consolidate his power. First, he would assume control of the building itself. On July 19, Burger, in shirt sleeves, assembled his law clerks and the marshal—the top administrative and business officer of the Court—for a tour of the large building.

Beginning in his own small office Burger remarked that it was smaller than his old one at the court of appeals. More distressing was the absence of an adjoining office that could be used as a workroom. As chief justice he was third in protocol as official representative of the United States government after the president and vice president. He would receive ambassadors and visiting dignitaries. "How can I entertain heads of state?" he asked, pointing to his relatively cramped quarters. It would never do. What would his guests think?

Passing through the secretaries' outer office, the procession stepped through to the most secret place of the Court, the conference room where the nine justices met to vote and decide cases. Few outsiders had seen the conference room during the Warren years. No person—clerk, staff member or secretary—was in attendance when the justices met, usually on Fridays, to discuss cases and take initial votes.

Burger surveyed this large, oak-paneled room and its rich carpet. A 12-foot-long table covered in green felt stood in the center of the room under a splendid chandelier, and was surrounded by nine handsome high-backed green leather swivel chairs. A brass nameplate on the back of each chair identified its occupant. The chief justice sat at one end of the table, the senior associate justice at the other. The other associates sat three on one side, four on the other. Now this room, the chief said, is perfect for entertaining guests. He told the group that in the original architect's plans, the room had been intended for the chief justice. Perhaps the conferences might be better in larger, more formal settings, the East and West conference rooms on the other side of the building. It might be more appropriate in that "neutral corner," Burger said. Then this room could become the chief justice's ceremonial office. He could also use it as a private dining room.

Next, Burger led the group across the corridor to the courtroom proper. They entered from behind the bench, as the justices did when they came to hear oral arguments or announce decisions. Burger stepped down to the pit in front of the mammoth bench. The large dignified room, with its dark-red curtains, had 24 marble columns rising 44 feet, cathedral-like, to a sculpted marble panel.

The new chief stepped to the podium from which the attorneys argued their cases to the nine justices—without witnesses and without introduction of evidence. Burger pointed to the justices' nine high-backed black leather chairs. Each justice chose his own, and the sizes and styles varied. It looked unseemly, disorderly,

Burger said. In the future only one kind of chair would be available. With the justices all in a straight line at a straight bench, they could not see or hear each other. That situation should be changed, he said, by curving the bench so each justice could see his colleagues. The acoustics in the large room also were poor. That too should be corrected, he said, perhaps by installing microphones. The clerks fidgeted.

They walked to the outer corridor on the first floor onto which each justice's suite of offices, known as *chambers*, faced. As they strolled along, Burger pointed out various problems—places in need of repainting, inadequate lighting. Burger concluded the Supreme Court Building with its fine workmanship, its columns, its brass doors and best wood was as grand as the White House, but it had not been kept up. A top-to-bottom reorganization was needed. The nineteenth-century administrative system might be charming, but it was inefficient. The tour lasted two hours.

Burger was happy with the way things were getting organized. He wanted to move his desk and other office furniture into the conference room and get settled in as quickly as possible. When the other justices returned, they would be confronted with a *fait accompli*. Burger's clerks were astonished that he would try such a move without consulting the others. He seemed to be moving toward a needless confrontation.*

Back at his office, Burger saw another opportunity to accomplish something where his predecessor had failed. Warren and his Court had alienated Congress over the years, particularly the

---

* Burger dropped his plan to make the conference room his ceremonial office when he learned through his clerks that the other justices were opposed. They felt the room was their sanctorum.

older, powerful, conservative committee chairmen, who didn't like the Court's decisions and resented Warren's aloofness.

Burger phoned Representative John Rooney, chairman of the House subcommittee that controlled the Court's spending. Warren had said privately that the crusty, gravel-voiced, 65-year-old Rooney was "dictatorial and vengeful." Burger decided to charm him. The Court needed more law clerks. Rooney told Burger that Warren had requested nine more, one for each justice. That was too many, Rooney said. Three might be a more reasonable request.

Three would be fine, Burger said.

Rooney said that as a special favor he would see if he could get the House to approve the three additional clerks.

Burger thanked Rooney for the effort.

Three days later, on July 14, the House approved three new clerks, and Rooney took to the floor to praise the new chief justice. The country, Rooney told his colleagues, "is in good hands when we are in the hands of Chief Justice Warren Burger."

At the Court, Burger told his clerks of his success. The lobbying and his willingness to compromise had paid off.

On July 29, Burger decided to make a move to put a damper on Warren's recent drive to impose a rigorous code of ethics for federal judges. Warren's original interest had gained some currency in the wake of the Fortas affair. But it was a tempest in a teapot, Burger said. He drafted a strong letter to the lower court judge who headed a committee that Warren had set up to formulate a code of ethics. Codes of ethics merely drew undue attention to minor problems, Burger wrote, and they gave the press more ammunition to depict judges as crooks.

Newspapers had published details about $6,000 in fees that Burger had received in the last three years as a trustee of the Mayo

Foundation, which operated the Mayo Clinic in Rochester, Minnesota. The ethics question had been overheated both by Warren and the press, Burger felt. He was determined to cool it off.

In early August, the chief turned his attention to selecting the three law clerks who were to be added to the Court. They were going to solve a problem—lack of staff. The Court was flooded each year with thousands of petitions from people who did not have attorneys and could not pay the $100 filing fee for review. The petitions might be jotted on notebook leaves or on scraps of paper. They were sometimes illegible and often incomprehensible.

These petitions constituted the bulk of the approximately 5,000 that came to the Court each year. They were called *in forma pauperis* petitions, or "IFPs." The Court got only one copy of each, rather than the 40 that were required of those able to pay. Most of the IFPs were from prisoners who alleged a violation of their constitutional rights. All the justices agreed that only a few petitions had merit, but Burger thought that all IFPs were a waste of time. In a 1965 court of appeals opinion *(Williams v. U.S.)*, he had denounced the "Disneyland" contentions of those who had been found guilty and were still trying to get out of jail by raising technical objections.

The office of the chief justice was responsible for these IFPs. Generally, the petitions themselves did not go to each justice. The chief's clerks wrote one-page summaries of each, and these were circulated to the other chambers. If the clerk who handled the petition believed the claim to be particularly meritorious, the whole petition might be circulated.

As he was getting the chief's chambers organized, Burger's head law clerk reviewed a copy of a 33-page set of instructions Warren had written for his law clerks that included a guide on how to prepare these IFP memos. Burger's clerk edited the guide and sent it to the chief for his okay.

Burger found no problems until he got to page 17, the section dealing with the clerks' responsibilities in preparing the summaries of the IFPs. Such summaries, the memo said, should pull together and accurately set forth the facts, issues and legal arguments that each petitioner had tried to make.

The chief called in his head clerk. What's this? Burger demanded. This was a court, not the office of the public defender. That might be the way Warren's clerks operated, but it was not what his would do, Burger stated firmly. The Court was already overworked. If some poor devil missed a point that might get his petition reviewed by the Court, well, that was his problem. In criminal cases, these people had already been found guilty and were looking for technicalities and loopholes to escape their just punishment. This secondary function would be *ignored*, Burger declared. Only arguments that had been identified by the petitioner would be summarized and sent to the other chambers.

Burger's clerks believed he had effectively devastated the Court's role as the last bastion of hope for these people. Without knowing any law, most petitioners had little chance of catching the Court's attention. The IFPs, however, were only one example, in Burger's view, of how law clerks had come to have too much power and influence.

He knew from his days at the court of appeals how clerks occasionally worked their little subterfuges. To combat this, he modified a memo on confidentiality from the previous term at the court of appeals. It was issued by his own senior clerk on August 12, only to his own law clerks.

The memo noted that during the year, there develops "a

communal professional life somewhat comparable to a large law firm." The various chambers, however, are not members of the same law firm, but rather different law offices coincidentally occupying the same building.

> Any matters of a confidential nature which tend to place the Chief Justice in an unfavorable light should not be revealed to other Law Clerks.
>
> Despite the avowed confidentiality of the lunchroom, the possibility of unfavorable information being "leaked" to other justices requires the Chief's Law Clerks to be reticent.

The chief was worried not about leaks to outsiders, but about his clerks telling tales that would "leak" to his colleagues.

The chief "does not want his views on a case—or those of his law clerk(s)—made known *outside* his Chambers until his final position is reached.

> The Chief's clerks are not to reveal which opinions they are personally working on. . . . The Chief Justice has a strict rule that suggestions are to be accepted from other offices *only* after another Justice has first considered the matter and then communicated directly and formally to the Chief Justice.

So they couldn't negotiate with the other clerks. No one could be told anything, and no other chambers would receive advance soundings on the chief's initial conclusions. They were to work under a bell jar, away from the flow of ideas and argument. The chief, they concluded, had a view of the Court that implied that such interchanges corrupted rather than enlightened. Their disaffection grew. It was as if the chief had prepackaged legal values and did not want the normal give-and-take to sway either him or his clerks. Even to Burger's clerks, the memo reflected his deep insecurity over control and a fear that somehow the clerks would try to manipulate him.

Burger had one more summer project. Earl Warren had feuded with and alienated the major organization of lawyers in the country, the American Bar Association. In 1958, the ABA convention held in London included a committee report condemning the Warren Court for comforting the Communists and treading on states' rights. Warren had responded by resigning from the association, becoming one of the few prominent lawyers in the country who were not members.

Resolved to reopen the lines of communication to the organized legal establishment, Burger attended the ABA's summer convention in Dallas. It could help him, and he could help it. He agreed to give four speeches. Introducing himself as "Warren Burger," he circulated through the crowds, hand outstretched. There was a message. A new "partnership" had been born among lawyers, judges and law professors, for so long considered separate components of the legal world, often with sharply differing views. The chief promised to attend ABA sessions "for the rest of my days."

After the convention, Burger flew to Los Angeles to attend a dinner that President Nixon was giving to honor the first astronauts to have walked on the moon.

———

At 83, Hugo Black was the Court's oldest associate justice and its senior member. Shriveled and slightly stooped, Black had for years amazed everyone with his vitality. He was about to begin his 32nd term in rather poor health.

Earlier in the summer, the appeals court had asked the U.S. Department of Health, Education and Welfare to submit desegregation plans for 33 school districts in Mississippi so it could order them implemented at the beginning of the school year. HEW was in charge of drawing up the plans as mandated under the 1964 Civil Rights Act, and had submitted them on time. At the last minute, however, both HEW and the Justice Department had asked for extensions until December 1, because, they claimed, the plans had been hastily prepared and would result in "chaos, confusion, and a catastrophic educational setback." It was the first time the federal government had supported a desegregation delay in the federal courts. To Black's astonishment and dismay, the Fifth Circuit had granted the delay, deferring to HEW's technical expertise. What was more, no specific date for implementing the plans for the actual desegregation had been set. Black saw this as part of the so-called "Southern Strategy" that had helped Nixon win the presidential election.

In spite of the Court's historic 1954 ruling *(Brown v. Board of Education I)* that segregated schools were unconstitutional, a great majority of schools in the Deep South had circumvented desegregation. Black had given in to Justice Felix Frankfurter's demand that the phrase "all deliberate speed" be included in the Court's 1955 ruling (*Brown v. Board of Education II*) to set the rate at which school systems must desegregate. A series of Supreme Court decisions during the last decade had nullified many of the evasive tactics that school boards had used to fight actual desegregation.

In September, Black received a memorandum from the Justice Department. Solicitor General Griswold was urging that Black permit the Mississippi delay. Griswold acknowledged that such a delay "means in most situations, another school year, and that is a tragedy and a default." But he argued that it was inevitable, because of the need to revamp student assignments and reschedule and reshuffle faculties.

Black found this request absurd. However, even though he had the authority and could do what he thought was proper, he wanted to avoid triggering a split in the Court. Black decided not to overturn the delay but to set forth his own views as strongly as possible and thus show the way for the Court. Black issued a five-page opinion that left the Fifth Circuit's delay intact, "deplorable as it is to me," and invited the NAACP Legal Defense and Educational Fund, Inc.—commonly known as the "Inc. Fund"— that was representing the Black people in Mississippi to "present the issue to the full Court at the earliest possible opportunity."

The opinion might force the Court to take the case. Since 1954, the Court had always been unanimous in school cases, its strong commands to desegregate joined by every member. For 15 years, the justices had agreed that it was essential to let the South know that not a single justice believed in anything less than full desegregation. To preserve that unanimity, the Court could not let the Fifth Circuit delay remain in force. Black's opinion put him on record as favoring a reversal.

The Inc. Fund followed Black's suggestion and filed an emergency petition asking for a prompt hearing. In October, the Justice Department formally urged the Court to use its discretionary power not to hear the case, arguing that it would be better to wait and see what the Mississippi schools did after the plans were

submitted on December 1. At conference, Black was able to mus-
ter the four votes required to grant the Inc. Fund cert petition.*
The justices agreed to put the case at the head of the docket and
to hear oral arguments in two weeks, on October 23.

The press followed the case closely. Justice Department officials were saying that a Court decision in favor of the Inc. Fund,
one that demanded immediate desegregation, would be tough to
enforce because the department did not have enough lawyers, and
because the South might react violently. The president remarked
at a press conference that those who wanted "instant integration"
were as "extremist" as those who wanted "segregation forever."
Lower federal court judges who were on the battle lines, with
hundreds of similar school cases before them, waited to see what
signal, if any, might be forthcoming.

On the morning of Thursday, October 23, the courtroom was
packed. Two hours, twice the normal time, had been allotted for
oral argument. Jack Greenberg, chief lawyer for the Inc. Fund,
opened. He said there had been enough stalling and enough law-
lessness by the Southern school officials. Greenberg wanted a
strong desegregate-at-once statement that would have a straight-
forward symbolic effect. He did not want the Court to focus on
the practical problems of ordering instant desegregation.

Mitchell had assigned the head of the Civil Rights Division

---

* A cert petition is a document filed with the Court, making the arguments as to why the justices should take a particular case for consideration.
Under the Court's internal rules, four votes—one less than a majority—
are required to accept a case. The term cert petition is used in this book to
refer both to *petitions for certiorari* and, in the case of appeals, to *statements
of jurisdiction*.

of the Justice Department, Jerris Leonard, to present the government's case. Leonard had barely given an account of the government's successes in achieving desegregation in the South when he was interrupted by questions, first from Douglas and then from Black. Trying to brush them off, Leonard stated that there were practical problems, that the situation was complicated.

"What's so complicated?" Black challenged testily.

Leonard backpedaled. "What I'm pleading with this Court is not to do something precipitous—"

That set Black off. "Could anything be precipitous in this field now?" He could not hide his contempt. "With all the years gone by since our order was given?"

Leonard continued, but he was interrupted repeatedly.

Burger's low baritone attempted to soothe the waters. "Just one question if I may. If there had been no appeal here . . . can you assure us that the plans would have been submitted on December 1?"

Leonard was happy with that question. Yes, he assured the chief. If the Court did nothing, the new plans would be submitted by then.

Burger was satisfied. It was already the end of October. Whether the Court overturned or upheld the lower court order, the plans would be submitted in about five weeks. But White and Black forced Leonard to concede that even if the plans were in by then, the latest appeals court decision did not guarantee that desegregation would take place before the next school year. Leonard admitted that another year might go by without much progress.

"Too many plans and not enough action," Black said with a thin smile, and the audience burst into laughter.

———

The next day, Friday, October 24, the justices met in conference to discuss the case. Tradition dictated that the chief speak first, that he outline the issues and briefly state his view. Then the discussion would proceed in order of seniority, starting with Black. Theoretically, voting would then take place in the opposite order, starting with the junior justice, Thurgood Marshall. But over a period of time, the formal vote had been dispensed with, since, in expressing his views, each justice let it be known where he stood. If his position was firm, it amounted to a vote.

The chief, sitting in his chair at the end of the table, turned to the Mississippi case, the first major case of the term. The crowded courtroom the day before, the intense press interest, the passion of the lawyers, and the obvious concern and emotion of his colleagues, suggested this case would be a landmark, an enduring guide for future cases of the same type. It might be the most important case since the original *Brown* decision. The Warren Court had built much of its reputation on 15 years of school desegregation cases. Now, Warren Burger, as chief justice, would guide the Court to its next milestone. It would be a test of his leadership. From what he had heard and seen, Burger realized that unanimity, the unwritten rule in these cases, was going to be difficult to achieve. His own position differed from Black's opinion. Burger didn't think the Justice Department was being wholly unreasonable. Clearly there were practical problems—problems HEW and the appeals court understood better than the Supreme Court—and it was important that the plans be workable.

Black, sitting as senior justice at the opposite end of the conference table, spoke next. Five weeks, he said, was not the issue. It was symbolic. Any willingness on the part of the Court to grant a delay, no matter how slight, would be perceived as a signal. To appear to waver, even for a second, would be a betrayal. Black attacked Nixon and his administration bitterly. They were allowing the South hope of further evasions. The Court must resolve the problem and reaffirm its commitment before Nixon took hold of the situation. What little progress there had been in the South and the Border States had really occurred after the Justice Department and HEW had stepped in to sue school boards and to draw up plans. The Court could not permit them to drop out of the struggle now.

All that was needed in this case was a short, simple order, Black argued, not an opinion. There had already been too much writing. Black wanted unanimity as much as anyone, but if the Court's order mentioned the word "plan," he would dissent. There must be nothing that school districts or the Nixon administration could grab on to for another round of quibbling. Black also agreed with the Inc. Fund that everyone seemed to have this matter all backwards. Everyone seemed to think that the status quo was segregation, and that monumental efforts had to be launched to change the status quo. But the law was the status quo. And the law, laid down 15 years before by this Court, called for single, unitary school systems. The order should explicitly reject "all deliberate speed" and demand desegregation immediately, today, at once, now. No more rhetoric.

Next it was Douglas's turn to speak. Back from a summer at Goose Prairie in the Cascade Mountains of Washington State, Douglas was an imposing physical presence in the conference. White-haired, with a cowlick, a sinewy six-footer, he looked uncomfortable in his inexpensive business suit, rumpled white dress shirt and Dacron tie. Tanned and weathered, his face reflected his many off-season trips to all parts of the world. His 20 books, countless articles and speeches, and even the cowboy dime novels published under a pen name in his youth reflected his individualistic values. Douglas had built his life on adversity: poverty, polio, camping accidents. He had spent most of his years moving against the grain. He had been twice mentioned as a vice-presidential candidate, and once he had been offered the nomination, but he had decided against a politician's life.

Douglas's soft voice countered his authoritative tone. He rarely spoke at length in conference. He had decided years before that attempts to persuade were futile, or, even worse, counterproductive. His colleagues knew where he stood on most issues. He unabashedly accepted liberal dogma. He was for the individual over government, government over big business, and the environment over all else. But Douglas still insisted on laying out his exact resolution of each element of a case in his formal written opinions. If he could not persuade his colleagues, he could at least spread his ideas outside the Court.

Douglas wanted the Court to move aggressively on the race issue. In typewriter cadence, he clicked off several sentences on his general position, moved to his next point, kicking the table as he paused, jumped to another point without a connective, flapped his ear nervously while staring coldly across the table, and finally, again without warning, tied up his first and last points in terse summation.

To the others, the position was clear. Douglas would support Black.

John Harlan, quietly chain-smoking Larks, had been scrupulously attentive during Black's tirade. One hand rested near his grandfather's gold watch chain strung across the vest of his dark suit. A Wall Street lawyer from a wealthy family, private schools, then Princeton and Oxford, John Harlan was the quint-essential patrician, generally unflappable and unfailingly courte-ous. Despite—and also because of—his near-blindness in the last few years, Harlan was the Court's hardest working member. No matter how insignificant the disagreement or how minor the case, Harlan felt compelled to spell out his views for the sake of intel-lectual honesty. He made one exception to that rule: school deseg-regation cases.

Harlan had been the "conservative conscience" of the Warren Court, a frequent dissenter. He advocated restraint rather than activism. Despite his disagreements with Black, the two were as close as brothers. Harlan felt that he understood Black's concerns, particularly his guilt and anguish over "all deliberate speed." Yet he was offended by Black's speech, not because of the attack on Nixon—that was just Hugo—but because an order was no way to decide a major case. It would be preposterous for the Court just to say "Do it now," without offering any reasoning. The district and appeals courts needed guidance, and that required an opinion.

Black was being too emotional. Ever since his stroke, Black had been increasingly unpredictable, testy and belligerent, Har-lan thought. "Difficult," Harlan called it. Black wanted to decide this case in a spasm of indignation. Harlan would not allow it. For years, internal disagreements had been festering among the justices on the difficult details of desegregation. They had subor-dinated those disagreements to maintain their united front. Har-lan felt that this might be the case where their differences might erupt into public view.

Harlan said he agreed that delay should be rejected out of hand in strong language, but in a well-reasoned opinion. But he was not going along with any notion of immediate desegregation.

Instant desegregation was impossible. Harlan also strongly disagreed with Black's notion that "all deliberate speed" was at the heart of the delays. Another phrase, or no phrase at all, would not have helped. He wanted unanimity, but if Black wrote a separate opinion, he too would write separately.

Brennan was disturbed to see the conference splintering. He agreed with much of what Black said, but one had to be practical. He wanted to stay in the middle. That had been his vantage point for years as the prime mover on the Warren Court. Physically smaller than his colleagues, Brennan was the most energetic advocate. He cajoled in conference, walked the halls constantly and worked the phones, polling and plotting strategy with his allies. He was thin and gray-haired, and his easy smile and bright blue eyes gave him a leprechaun's appearance as he sidled up and threw his arms around his colleagues. His warmth allowed Brennan alone to call the reserved Harlan "Johnny." It had been Brennan who had sat each Thursday with Warren preparing an orchestration for the Friday conference.

"Well, guys, it's all taken care of," Brennan often told his clerks after the sessions with Warren. With votes from Fortas, Marshall and usually Douglas, Brennan rarely failed to put together a majority. He had dissented only three times the previous term, only 30 times in the last half decade. Now, with Burger replacing Warren and Black threatening to dissent, the situation looked bleak. So Brennan said little.

Potter Stewart spoke, and then Byron White. Both were upset by Black's threat, and his absolutist position. The school year had already begun. The Court had to recognize that. They both believed that the intricate processes of desegregating schools couldn't be accomplished over a weekend.

Stewart had been an appeals court judge before coming to the Court. He wanted to help the lower courts, not to confuse them. Black's "now" view might make good reading, but the trial courts needed to know what to do. If the Court said "now," the appeals and district court judges would simply ask, "What does that mean?" Worse, Stewart feared that the lower courts would lose faith in the Supreme Court if it came out with some abstract pronouncement.

There was no question where the final speaker at conference, Thurgood Marshall, stood on the question of school desegregation. Marshall had headed the Inc. Fund for 22 years, from its founding in 1939 until 1961, when John F. Kennedy appointed him to the Second Circuit Court of Appeals. The great-grandson of a slave, son of the steward at a fashionable all-White Chesapeake Bay yacht club, Marshall pioneered the civil rights battle against segregation in housing, public accommodations and schools. He won 29 of the 32 cases he argued before the Supreme Court for the Inc. Fund.

In 1965, Lyndon Johnson appointed Marshall solicitor general. When Marshall hesitated, Johnson's closing argument was, "I want folks to walk down the hall at the Justice Department and look in the door and see a nigger sitting there." Two years later Johnson appointed Marshall to the Supreme Court. Marshall had not sought and had not wanted the appointment. He preferred the more active give-and-take of public-interest law. His jurisprudence was long settled; so at conference, Marshall was relaxed, almost intuitively reaching his commonsense solution. He had fit easily into the Warren liberal majority. Plainspoken and direct, Marshall saw his job as casting his vote and urging his colleagues to do what was right. On the Court, he had little interest in perfecting the finer points of the law. He often told his clerks, only half jokingly, "I'll do whatever Bill [Brennan] does," sometimes even jotting "follow Bill" on his notes. He trusted Brennan's resolution of the detailed, technical questions of legal scholarship. The clerks had taken to calling Marshall "Mr. Justice Brennan-Marshall." Often he would follow White on antitrust cases. But on discrimination cases, Marshall followed no one.

Marshall had headed the team of lawyers who argued the original *Brown* cases. He remained unhappy with "all deliberate speed." He shifted his massive 6-foot-1, 250-pound body slightly as he closed in on his point. He agreed with Black that the phrase was ill-chosen. But the most important element in this case was unanimity for desegregation. There must be no suggestion that the Court was backtracking. He was a practical man. If necessary, he said, he was willing to go along with a delay to December 1 for submission of plans.

But that was not the major point. Marshall was concerned with bread-and-butter issues—getting Black kids and White kids in the same schools. The key was a date for implementation of the plans, and the Fifth Circuit had not set one. Without a date, even the Justice Department admitted that implementation would not occur until the next school year. Surely the schools could do better than that, Marshall said. He proposed setting the implementation deadline for January, the beginning of the next semester.

———

As the justices expressed their views, Burger grew increasingly worried. The new chief had seen during his first weeks that many cases were not decided at conference. Feelings were tentative, disagreements subtle. Often, something had to be put down on paper before a consensus emerged. Burger knew the press would view this case as the first test of his leadership. None of the opinions argued so far was nearly ready to be issued. Burger didn't want to let things get any more out of control than they already were.

The justices did have some points of agreement. First, the Supreme Court itself must not appear to be delaying. An expedited order would have to be issued soon—perhaps by the coming week. Second, the court of appeals should retain jurisdiction and, thus, control. The federal district court, which had allowed years of stalling, should not be involved. There even appeared to be a majority for reversing the appeals court's decision to grant a delay in the submission of plans. So that issue was settled. But beyond these points, there was a broad spectrum of opinion on what the Court should do and say. Should the Court set specific deadlines for the appeals court, or allow it some flexibility to work out the problem?

In keeping with the tradition that the chief justice assigns opinions if he is a member of the majority, Burger said he would try to work out language in a simple order that would encompass the concerns of all the justices. That could be followed by a full opinion if they all agreed to it.

The way Burger analyzed the conference discussion, the main obstacle to a unanimous decision was Black. Douglas was following his lead. They were alone in insisting that the Court should order desegregation now and that no opinion should be written, points on which even Brennan and Marshall seemed open to compromise. If they could be kept from joining Black, then Black would almost certainly back down, despite his rhetoric in conference.

After the conference, Burger met with Harlan and Stewart

and asked for their help. They had been through this process before, working with widely disparate views, attempting to reach a common ground. Burger asked Harlan if he would draft a possible order for the Court to issue. He wanted Harlan's thoughts as a starting point.

Harlan went to his chambers to work. Normally, he would have a clerk prepare a first draft. This one he did himself. His grandfather's picture looked down on him from the wall opposite his desk. Harlan's face almost touched the paper as he pushed a ballpoint pen across the pad. The writing was hardly legible.

"Proposed Order and Judgment," he wrote at the top.

"The question presented is one of paramount importance. . . . In view of the gravity of the issues and the exigency of prompt compliance with the Constitution, we deem it appropriate to enter the following order." He paused and added, ". . . with the opinion of the Court to follow this order." There simply had to be an opinion.

"The Court of Appeals . . . is reversed," he wrote, saying that the court of appeals should determine "forthwith" if the original HEW plans were "adequate and reasonable interim means"— that was for realists like himself—"to achieve immediate desegregation." That last phrase was for Black.

But when should the order be implemented? The question had been left up in the air at conference. It wasn't clear that a single deadline could be set. Some school systems might be able to desegregate immediately.

"The earliest possible moment," Harlan wrote, adding, "and in no event later than _____ ___, _____." He left blanks. An outer limit probably should be set, perhaps midyear, but there had been no consensus.

The two-page order was immediately sent down to the Court's printing shop in the basement. Even the most tentative drafts were generally printed and copies distributed to the other chambers. Early printed drafts in cases were never released, only the final ones.

The next morning, Saturday, October 25, most of the justices came to the Court. Black stayed home.

The chief asked Harlan and White to his chambers to go over Harlan's draft. Burger and White had also drafted possible orders. With a few changes, however, Harlan's draft served as the basis for their agreement.

———

When Brennan, Marshall and Douglas reviewed the proposed order, they agreed that it simply was not strong enough. The order would have to be improved before they could find it palatable, and certainly it was not going to be acceptable to Black. Marshall had been willing to compromise as long as there was an implementation deadline that insured desegregation by the next semester. But now he thought Black might be right. His insistence on "now" might be unreasonable, but it was quite likely the Court's best posture.

Marshall was also concerned that he would end up on the wrong side of a Black dissent. He did not want to be in a position where another member of the Court was claiming that he, of all people, was backing down. What the newspapers said the day after the Court issued its decision would be important. Marshall had to protect his position. He instructed his clerks to begin work on an opinion. At the same time, he did not want to lose touch with the others, so he sent one of his two clerks to talk with Harlan's clerks, to see if some compromise could be reached.

Meanwhile, Brennan decided that he too had to do something. Black, Douglas, Marshall and he could not let the more conservative quartet of Burger, Harlan, Stewart and White control the outcome by having the only drafts in circulation.* In phone conversations with Black, Brennan became convinced that Black was adamant. The collective liberal position would have to be largely Black's if they were going to act as a bloc. Black's view was appealing. The Court had to be tough and dramatic, perhaps a little unreasonable, in order not to appear to be buckling.

After talking it over with Douglas and Marshall, Brennan threw himself into composing a draft order. He wrote that desegregation according to the "all deliberate speed" standard "is no longer Constitutionally permissible. The obligation of the federal courts is to achieve desegregation . . . NOW." The HEW plans could be used if they achieve desegregation "immediately." Desegregation was the status quo.

In order to expedite action, Brennan wrote, the court of appeals "is requested so far as possible and necessary, to lay aside all other business of the court to carry out this mandate." Such a request from the Supreme Court was unusual. It would impress everyone with the urgency of the matter and the extent of the Court's commitment.

Black was home on Sunday, October 26, 1969, studying the chief's proposed order. He thought it awful. He liked Brennan's proposal, which reflected his own arguments from conference two days earlier. Perhaps the others had not taken his threat to write a dissent seriously. Black decided that he had better make

---

* It was still an eight-man Court since no replacement for Fortas had been confirmed by the Senate.

good on his word, and he began writing. Beginning with a history of the *Brown* decision, renewing his attack on "all deliberate speed," Black scrawled his message across a yellow legal pad in large crooked letters: "It is almost beyond belief that the factors mentioned by this Court in *Brown II*, to permit some slight delay in 1954, are precisely the same considerations relied upon in this case to justify yet another delay in 1969."

> The time has passed for plans and promises to desegregate. The Court's order here, however, seems to be written on the premise that schools can dally along with still more and more plans. The time for such delay I repeat we have already declared to be gone. . . .
> I would have the Court issue the following order.

Black attached a copy of Brennan's order.

In case anyone missed the import of what he was doing, Black drafted a cover memo emphasizing his intent to dissent. He had it sent to the Court and printed, with a copy for each justice.

The chief was alarmed at Black's memo and his threatened dissent. If the Court's unanimity broke apart on a school case, particularly so early in his tenure, he would be declared an instant failure. For the sake of unanimity, he would go along with anything they could all agree on.

The next two days were a whirl of paper. Drafts and counterdrafts of proposed orders flew from chamber to chamber as the justices added their thoughts. The main actors were the chief, Stewart, Harlan, Brennan and Marshall. Black and Douglas had apparently decided on their view. White was leaving most of the work to the others. His main concern was unanimity.

The eight-man Court seemed deadlocked 4 to 4. Black, Douglas, Brennan and Marshall were on one side, agreeing on immediate desegregation and no full Court opinion. On the other side were Burger, Harlan, Stewart and White trying for something firm but less absolute, more practical, more sympathetic to the concerns of the Executive Branch.

One by one, they decided that they might as well give in and join Brennan. It was more important that the Court be unanimous, perhaps just as important that they act that week, to emphasize their commitment to desegregation. By the end of the day all four had approved the Brennan order with a few changes in wording. There would be no full opinion to follow.

Black had won every major point. "All deliberate speed" was declared over, "no longer Constitutionally permissible." No delay would be permitted. In effect, the Court ruling said that the deadline had passed 15 years ago. The final opinion stated, "The obligation of every school district is to terminate dual school systems at once and to operate now and hereafter only unitary schools." The Fifth Circuit was directed to issue its order "effective immediately." The HEW plans could be used insofar as they helped achieve immediate and total desegregation.

Stewart thought the case was a demonstration of the new chief's inability to lead them through a crisis. The Court's reputation was a result of its bold desegregation decisions, and Burger had done nothing to sustain that reputation. Stewart felt that Earl Warren would have explained to Black that no one was going to dissent, period, and that they would all work something out. Black would never have pulled such a stunt with Warren.

Burger was elated that the decision was unanimous.

The next morning, Wednesday, October 29, six days after oral arguments, the decision was announced. The news stories noted that the decision was a setback for the Nixon administration—the end of dual school systems, and without further delay. Senator Strom Thurmond of South Carolina decried the decision, while praising the president. "The Nixon Administration stood with the South in this case."

The new Court under Burger, declared former Alabama governor George Wallace, was "no better than the Warren Court"; the justices were a bunch of "limousine hypocrites."

One of Burger's clerks congratulated him on standing up to the administration, saying this case would show the country that the chief wasn't Nixon's puppet. Burger was flabbergasted. "Do you think people really think I'm a Nixon puppet?"

At the White House, the president and his strategists were content. Nixon had lined up his administration squarely in favor of reasonable delay. The Supreme Court had said no more delay. Elections could be won or lost on the question. White Southerners would be enraged by the decision, but it was the Court's fault, not his.

Nixon's Southern Strategy suffered another defeat a few weeks later. The president had nominated conservative South Carolinian Clement F. Haynsworth, Jr., chief judge of the Fourth Circuit Court of Appeals, to fill Fortas's seat on the Supreme Court. But the liberals—by then recovered from the shock of the Fortas affair—had counterattacked.

Labor and civil rights groups opposed the confirmation, shrilly denouncing Haynsworth's opinions as consistently anti-union and against school desegregation. The liberals picked up the support of moderate Republicans when it was discovered that Haynsworth had participated in a case indirectly involving a company in which he held stock. It wasn't a major conflict of interest, according to experts who testified. But, added to the raw political opposition to Haynsworth, it was enough to tilt the votes against him. On November 21, the Senate rejected Haynsworth's nomination 55 to 45.

Burger had been looking forward to the arrival of a conservative vote that might help him shift the Court's direction. He blamed the White House for mishandling the nomination. Haynsworth was a victim of Washington's "jungle" politics, Burger told his clerks.

For the Court, the defeat meant more months without a ninth justice. Numerous petitions for Supreme Court review were pending. Four votes were needed before the Court would take a case, and dozens of cases were on hold because they had only three votes. They had been put in a "Hold for Haynsworth" file, to see if he would cast the fourth vote. Now the file was renamed "Hold for Justice X." The number of petitions waiting there grew each day.

———

It was late one Friday afternoon, and Burger was exhausted. A grueling, day-long conference had just ended. Unlike his colleagues, the chief couldn't now go home immediately. He had to make sure that the conference actions on the approximately 100 cert petitions that the justices considered each week were given to the Court's administrative personnel. Burger hated this chore. It was work proper for a clerk or a secretary, not for a chief justice. Since no one other than the justices was allowed in the conference room, he had to do it alone.

After each Friday conference, Burger would call in a law

clerk, a secretary and the clerk of the Court. Seated at his ceremonial desk in the conference room, they would go over the results. Three times early in the term, the published orders had incorrectly identified cases that had been accepted for full review. In fact, the petitions had been denied, and so public retractions had had to be made. The press had noticed the errors. The chief's secretary and his law clerks had tried to help by preparing elaborate briefing books, so that the chief had only to fill in the blanks with check marks. But it didn't seem to solve the problem. He was still making mistakes.

"Any dumb ass could pick it up," the chief's secretary once remarked privately.

After the votes had been given to the clerk of the Court, Burger went into his working office to finish another task, one he enjoyed. The chief spread a large sheet of plain butcher paper in front of him on the desk. Across the top were listed the names of the justices. Down the left side were the names of the cases heard so far that term. The sheet was Burger's most powerful tool in controlling the Court. It represented the workload of each justice. By tradition, the senior justice in the majority at conference selected the justice who was to write the Court opinion for the majority. Since the chief was considered senior to all the others, he made the assignments when he was in the majority. Burger was careful, in his first term, to make sure that he was in the majority most of the time—even if he had to adjust his views. Leadership in the Court could not be exercised from a minority position, he felt.

Since the chief assigned most of the cases, he was also responsible for keeping the majority-opinion assignments as evenly divided as possible. With only about 120 cases that required full opinions, including several that were unsigned *per curiams*, the power to select the author—to choose, for example, Harlan or Stewart instead of Brennan or Marshall—was the power to determine the general direction of the opinion. Often, the reasoning was as important as the finding itself. The lower courts would draw on the opinion for guidance as they made their decisions. Burger reasoned that by assigning the cases, he—as Warren had done before him—could control the Court and influence the entire federal judiciary. The process would take years, and it would have to be done a step at a time. But each assignment that he controlled was an important step.

Burger carefully made sure that important cases in criminal law, racial discrimination and free speech were kept away from Douglas, Brennan and Marshall, his ideological "enemies," as he called them. If necessary, the chief would switch his own vote to retain the assignment power, thus preventing them from writing groundbreaking decisions that expanded the Court's power or extended the application of liberal Warren Court decisions. Instead, he assigned them innocuous cases where their opinions couldn't have much impact.

Of those most likely to share his views, the chief at first found Byron White the most compatible. White was also the most physically impressive. At 6-feet-2 and a trim 190 pounds, he was still like the tough University of Colorado football All-American. White won a Rhodes Scholarship and then entered Yale Law School, where he passed up *Law Review* to earn money as the highest-paid professional football player of his day. Stewart, a classmate at law school, often saw White in the library in his steel-rimmed glasses, only to read about him in the next day's paper as the game-winning "Whizzer White." To Stewart and his classmates, White was both Clark Kent and Superman.

White clerked a year at the Court for Chief Justice Fred Vinson, and renewed his friendship with freshman Representative John Kennedy, whom he had known in England and later in the South Pacific during World War II. White's 15 years of law practice in Denver ended when he ran a nationwide Citizens for Kennedy committee during the 1960 presidential campaign. He was rewarded with the post of deputy attorney general as the number two man in Robert Kennedy's Justice Department. A year later, President Kennedy appointed White to the Court, saying that White "had excelled in everything he had attempted."

White was an aggressive justice, relentlessly pressing his clerks to clarify their own, and thus his own, arguments. Never relaxed, always competitive, White loved to race his clerks to complete the first draft of an opinion, or to interrupt them for a basketball game on the Court's fourth-floor gymnasium, which the clerks called "the highest court in the land."

White's positions were clear and vehement. They seemed to his colleagues to come directly out of his practical experience in the Justice Department. He was tough on the enforcement of both civil rights and criminal justice. And it was this last hard line that delighted Burger. The press repeatedly pointed to White as a disappointment to the liberals. Poker-faced, sometimes harsh, but confident and capable in the law, White was only 52 and likely to be an influence on the Court for years to come. Even when they disagreed on criminal cases, Burger could count on White to write an opinion reasonably close to his own views. Burger put a check under White's name for a criminal-case assignment.

The law clerk working with Burger was puzzled. Burger was in the minority on that one, the clerk reminded him; therefore, the assignment was not his to make.

Burger checked his vote book. No he was not in the minority, he replied.

"But before going to conference you said you would not vote that way," the clerk said.

"I never said such a thing," Burger said crisply.

Once, the clerk of the Court approached one of the chief's clerks. "I've been meaning to ask you something for a week," he said. "I often find my recollection differs from the chief's. Does yours?" Burger's law clerk said he was familiar with the problem and recalled some stories about conference votes and record keeping.

No, the clerk of the Court said, he knew about that. But he was talking about the chief's habit of reminiscing and placing himself at the center of events—saying things, doing things and making decisions all of which had been said, done or made by someone else.

After White, the chief felt most ideologically compatible with Harlan, then Stewart, and in some cases Black. After so many years as a leading liberal, Black had in recent years become increasingly conservative. He was living proof that events were pushing people to the political right, the chief felt. Liberalism was an experiment that had largely failed, and now one of the archliberals was moving back to common sense. Potter Stewart's initial optimism about the new regime had faded. One of his clerks, a committed liberal, had observed Burger in action at the District of Columbia Court of Appeals the previous year. He had sent early and repeated warnings to Stewart, characterizing Burger as petty, unpleasant and dishonest.

Stewart didn't want to jump to conclusions. He just laughed nervously as his clerks told new and old Burger tales, which always painted the chief in the worst possible light. But as the term progressed and Stewart compared notes with the other justices, particularly with his friend Harlan, his reservations about Burger turned to acute distress.

It occurred to Stewart that Burger was much like Earl Warren, inclined to shoot from the hip, or to view cases in purely political terms. In some respects, Burger was worse. He would go out of his way—bend the law, overlook earlier Court decisions—to hold a majority to keep someone in jail. But, unless the chief could get at least one other justice to go along with his hard-line views, he invariably moved toward the center, joining the most conservative position available. Stewart's clerks, and a number of others, worked out a theory of Burger's jurisprudence. The chief would never be alone in dissent. "Always to the right but never alone," the slogan went.

———

On Wednesday, April 8, 1970, Stewart returned from lunch shortly after 1 p.m. About 10 people, including Thurgood Marshall and one of Burger's secretaries, were clustered about a small black-and-white portable television in his secretary's office. They were watching reports of the Senate vote on Nixon's second attempt to fill the Fortas seat. The nominee was Judge G. Harrold Carswell, now a member of the Fifth Circuit Court of Appeals.

Stewart was not aware that Burger, before his own nomination to be chief justice, had suggested to Mitchell that Carswell be promoted from a district to an appeals court judge. Carswell's nomination, like Haynsworth's, had run into difficulties. It had been disclosed that Carswell had said in a 1948 speech that, "Segregation of the races is proper and the only practical and correct way of life in our states. I have always so believed and I shall always so act." He had renounced the speech, but it had triggered a search into his past. The search revealed that Carswell had been involved in a plan to use a federally financed public golf course in Florida as a private segregated club. His judicial and civil rights record also came under attack. Some legal scholars also stated that he was not fit to sit on the Supreme Court. During the vote, two key Republicans voted against the confirmation. The final tally was 51 to 45.

The next day, Nixon asserted angrily: "I will not nominate another Southerner and let him be subjected to the kind of malicious character assassination accorded both Judges Haynsworth and Carswell." The speculation among the justices and the clerks turned to what Nixon would do now. Who would be his non-Southerner?

————

Harry A. Blackmun, a veteran of 11 years' service on the Eighth Circuit Court of Appeals, was at work in his office in Rochester, Minnesota, the morning after Carswell's defeat in the Senate. At 11:05 a.m., the phone rang. It was Attorney General John Mitchell. "Can you get to D.C. and meet me at 9 a.m. tomorrow?" Mitchell asked.

The next day at 11:15 a.m., Blackmun arrived at Mitchell's office at the Justice Department. The grilling began. Mitchell was determined to learn everything about his latest nominee. There would be no more surprises. He wanted to know if there were skeletons. He quizzed Blackmun about his finances, his social activities, his writings, and his appeals court decisions.

Assistant Attorney General Rehnquist, head of Mitchell's personal legal staff at the Justice Department—the Office of Legal

Counsel—joined them. He was followed two hours later by John-
nie M. Walters, the head of the Department's tax division. There
would be no mistakes this time. Any area of possible trouble had
to be identified.

There were some minor difficulties. Blackmun held $2,500
and $1,350 of stock in two companies, and he had ruled on cases
indirectly involving them. Insubstantial as Blackmun's holdings
were, Haynsworth had been hurt by disclosure of such alleged
conflicts. It was decided that Walters would accompany Blackmun to Minnesota to gather the records. Everything had to be
made public before or right after the announcement of the nomination.

That afternoon Mitchell and Blackmun went to see the president at the White House. Nixon had not met with Haynsworth
or Carswell before their nominations, but he wanted to see Blackmun. Nixon found Blackmun's moderate conservatism perfect.
A short, modest, soft-spoken man, Blackmun had been Phi Beta
Kappa at Harvard, had gone on to Harvard Law School, a clerkship at the Eighth Circuit, 16 years of private practice, and about
10 years as general counsel to the famous Mayo Clinic. After that
he had been appointed to the Eighth Circuit by Eisenhower. He
had academic credentials, practical legal experience in the Middle
West, and a predictable, solid body of opinions that demonstrated
a levelheaded strict-constructionist philosophy. And Burger
thought highly of Blackmun. Blackmun was a decent man, con-
sistent, wedded to routine, unlikely to venture far.

Neither Nixon nor Mitchell asked Blackmun about his judicial philosophy. The judge had three daughters in their twenties.
Nixon asked if any were "hippie types." Blackmun assured him
that none was.

He saw his lifelong friendship with Burger as his greatest potential problem. They had gone to grade school together, and Blackmun was best man at Burger's wedding in 1933. After Burger came to Washington in 1953, they corresponded, and they saw each other when Burger came to Minnesota to visit his family.

"Look," Nixon said, "you two grew up together. Your paths separated when you went to different high schools. But you have remained good friends. I don't see anything wrong with that." He wanted to go ahead. The administration was ready for an offensive. A detailed financial report on Blackmun was released to the Senate Judiciary Committee.

Nina Totenberg, who covered the Supreme Court for the weekly newspaper the *National Observer*, was one of Washington's most aggressive reporters, unwilling to settle for the usually placid Court coverage. A specialist in digging out behind-the-scenes detail, Totenberg flew to Minneapolis to interview Blackmun's eighty-five-year-old mother. Mrs. Blackmun told Totenberg that the chief justice and her son talked to each other on the telephone almost once a week. They talked about all sorts of things, legal, political.

In an article Totenberg wrote that Mrs. Blackmun had recounted how once, the previous year, the chief justice had issued an open invitation to her son, "telling him that any time he needed assistance in sorting out recent Supreme Court decisions, he, the chief justice, would be glad to help. But Judge Blackmun, says Mrs. Blackmun, quickly declined the invitation, making it clear to the chief justice that he did not think receiving such assistance would be proper."

Blackmun was enraged at Totenberg. His relationship with Burger was the thing he was most sensitive about. For a moment, he considered withdrawing from the nomination. But Blackmun was ready when he faced Eastland's Senate committee on April 29. He was tense, but determined to be candid. He knew the key was to show no arrogance, to be self-effacing. It came naturally to him.

Blackmun was in Minnesota on the day of the final vote. He was trying to finish his appeals court work when two large canvas bags of cert petitions arrived from Washington. Burger soon called. "Did you get your mail?" he asked.

"Yes," Blackmun said jovially. "What's the idea?"

"You've got to go to work."

"I've got plenty of work out here," Blackmun said jokingly. "You're not my boss yet."

Burger wanted him in Washington before the term ended the next month. After a full year with only eight justices, nearly 200 petitions for review had been held for "Justice X." In many of these cases, there were three votes to grant a hearing and Blackmun could supply the fourth. On cases that questioned the constitutionality of the death penalty, the feeling had been that the Court should not even grant a hearing until it was certain there would be nine members to review the cases.

Blackmun was overwhelmed at the prospect of making so many important decisions. When he was working on the appeals court, there was always another review authority, the Supreme Court, to correct any mistake he might make. Now, on these 200 cases, it would be solely up to him. Blackmun was very cautious in dealing with the pending cert petitions. Burger did not want to take many of the cases. Blackmun finally voted to grant hearings in only three or four. Brennan was disappointed and concluded Burger had another vote.

Blackmun had arrived at the busiest time of the year, the "June crunch," when the undecided votes in dozens of cases were finally cast and the results announced. These cases were often the most important and difficult to decide, the justices having wrangled over them much of the term. By tradition and informal agreement, the Court tried to take final action on each of the argued cases before the end of the term. A decision might be issued. A case might be *dismissed as improvidently granted*—meaning that a majority had decided, at times even after oral argument, and often for technical reasons, not to decide the case. Or a case might be put over for reargument the next term. This year there were 16 cases put over for reargument, an unusually high number.

Blackmun sat quietly at the last conferences. He had not participated in the hearings, so he could not vote. No one said anything about it to him directly, but he soon realized that they were putting over most of the cases because the vote was deadlocked 4 to 4. His vote would decide most of them.

1970 TERM

AS HIS SECOND TERM APPROACHED, BURGER WOR-
ried increasingly about how his tenure would measure up against
Earl Warren's. In Warren's first term, the Court had handed down
the *Brown* school desegregation ruling. Over the next 16 years, his
monumental reputation for leadership and integrity had rested in
large part on the continuing chain of school desegregation cases.

For his part, Blackmun wasn't having an easy time adjusting
to the demands of the Court. At the Eighth Circuit Court of Appeals, he had used his clerks solely for mundane legal research.
Blackmun had started to use his clerks the same way on the Supreme Court, but soon expanded their role slightly. On one occa-
sion, he asked a clerk to research a question on jurisdiction and,
as was customary, then circulated the resulting memo in his own
name. It had barely left Blackmun's hands when a blistering response came in from Douglas, picking the legal research apart for
overlooking obvious points. Douglas's memo was almost sadistic.

Blackmun was mortified. He realized that Douglas was right.
He vowed to never again let his clerks be in a position to embarrass
him in front of his colleagues. His clerks once more received very
routine assignments, and Blackmun checked their work carefully.

More than anything, however, Blackmun often seemed

paralyzed by indecision. The problem was greatest on cases where his was the swing vote.

As Harlan left the bench one day early in the term, he overheard Brennan discussing a crucial case *(Younger v. Harris et al.)* with Blackmun. It had been held over for three straight years because the conference was deadlocked on the question of the power of federal courts to intervene in state court proceedings. Harlan, uncomfortable with lobbying, jokingly suggested to Brennan, "Why don't we let Harry confer by himself on these and we'll go back and get some work done."

Black also was concerned about Blackmun. "If he doesn't learn to make up his mind, he's going to jump off a bridge someday," Black remarked to his clerks. Black tried to help, and he would occasionally wander down the hall to Blackmun's chambers to provide encouragement. "Now Harry," Black once said, "you just can't agonize over it. You have just got to vote."

But Blackmun plodded along, working day and night, trying to master the record in each case, and read all previous Court decisions in every given area. Blackmun not only couldn't see the forest but was overwhelmed by each tree, Black figured. On one case in which he had voted to join Blackmun's dissent, Black walked down to see how Blackmun was doing. He found his colleague working away as usual, with piles of law books spread all over. Black looked over the work. "That's the way to it, Harry," he said. "Strike for the jugular, strike for the jugular."

The long delays were strategically bad for Blackmun. As he struggled to get out his views, other justices filed theirs and moved on to new cases. His influence was slight. When he first arrived, Blackmun warned Burger that they would be tagged the "Minnesota Twins" after the baseball team for their hometowns—the

Twin Cities of St. Paul and Minneapolis. It took only half a year of voting together before Blackmun's prophecy came true. He was only surprised it had taken so long.

Still, it particularly offended him, because the notion implied that Blackmun had no judicial mind of his own. But the fact remained that he and Burger had found themselves on opposing sides only twice in the first 50 cases decided by the Court. He never seemed to disagree with the chief when it really counted. The clerk network had another name for Blackmun: "Hip pocket Harry." Burger, they felt, controlled not only his own vote but Blackmun's as well.

———————

Burger brooded about his public image as a "conservative." The press liked to label justices as conservatives, liberals or moderates. That was understandable, Burger felt. Most people needed the shorthand, because they didn't read opinions or study the Court. But the labels were misleading and unfair. He didn't think of himself as a conservative. The press had cast him in that role, comparing him unfavorably with their hero Earl Warren. Burger thought of himself as moderate. Warren had been an "activist." Burger was determined to correct his image, to vote with the liberal wing, to write some "liberal" opinions. That, he confided to his clerks, would confuse his liberal detractors in the press.

"I have no plans to retire or not to retire," Black told reporters at a press conference two days before his 85th birthday in February 1971. Such questions were becoming more frequent. He was serving his 33rd year on the Court. Only four justices had served longer.

Privately, Black had been giving the notions of retirement and death considerable thought. As the term moved into the spring, Black's health deteriorated. Black began to stumble badly in conference, unable to remember which case they were on. He bitterly rejected Burger's suggestion, however, that the conferences end a bit earlier to accommodate him.

As the end of the term approached, Black's health continued to deteriorate. One day during the last week in May, he was returning to his chambers following conference when his knees buckled. By the time his clerks reached him and carried him into his office, he was shivering with a high fever. "They are after all my old majorities," he babbled as his clerks wrapped him in a blanket.

Black recovered from the fever, but his strength was seriously depleted. Disabling headaches plagued him, and his cheerful whistle as he strolled through the marble halls was suddenly missing.

For Black, who advocated positive thinking as the cure for every malady, the idea that he was no longer in full control of his own destiny was torture. For years, he had talked of how Oliver Wendell Holmes, Louis Brandeis and Benjamin Cardozo had lingered on at the Court, unable to perform their work competently. But Black was determined to remain. He had resisted Warren's and then Douglas's hints that he resign, and he had done his best to ignore Harlan's remarks that perhaps they both had stayed on too long. Now, in his 34th term, he had kept on his desk a small card bearing the exact lengths of service of John Marshall and Stephen J. Field. Both had served 34 terms and he would surpass both in a few months. But, finally, he was no longer sure that he could hold out.

Part II

_____

PRESENTING THE CASE

1971 TERM

IN LATE AUGUST 1971, THE CHIEF INVITED HIS NEW
clerks to join him for lunch. It was a last-minute invitation. Several
arrived at the ground-floor Ladies Dining Room carrying their
cafeteria lunches on trays. Since they had come to the Court at various times over the summer, Burger's clerks had had only fleeting
contact with their boss.

Alvin Wright, the chief's messenger and valet, stood in the
doorway wearing a white waiter's jacket. The sight of the familiar
messenger dressed as a waiter was startling enough, but suddenly
Wright pivoted and snapped to attention. "The Chief Justice of
the United States of America," he called out.

By reflex, the clerks rose.

"You've got to be shitting me," one mumbled in the face of a
hostile stare from Burger's senior clerk.

Burger strolled into the room, greeted each clerk graciously,
and took his place at the head of the table. The antique table was
covered with a linen cloth and set with the Court Historical Society's china and silver. Here in this dining room with pale-yellow
walls covered with portraits of the wives of the former chief justices, Burger felt comfortable. He had taken a great interest in
the proper refurbishing of this room. Newly acquired antiques,

financed through the Society with donations from prominent Washingtonians and members of the bar, were selected by the chief with great care. The room itself was a vestige of an age when the Court's oral arguments were among Washington's premier social events attended by the justices' wives and their guests.

Burger began this gathering with an introduction to the approaching term. Lamenting the fact that both John Harlan and Hugo Black had recently been hospitalized, he told some anecdotes about the warm affection that existed between these ideological opponents. He emphasized his respect and admiration for the two legal giants.

The chief also expressed concern about Marshall's recent emergency appendectomy. Marshall had not allowed the news media to know about complications that had arisen from a stomach ulcer. And though Douglas was healthy, he had had his heart pacemaker batteries replaced three months before. The message was clear.

Black had checked into the Bethesda Naval Medical Center for four days in mid-July and returned for two more days of tests later in the month. Despite his doctor's conclusions to the contrary, Black was certain that he had cancer. He had lost his appetite and weighed barely 115 pounds when his doctors asked his family to bring him back to the hospital in mid-August. Two days before he entered, he asked a former clerk, Lou Oberdorfer, a prominent Washington attorney, to draft a letter of resignation. Oberdorfer brought a copy to Black the next night. Black left the date open, but he signed it. "This," he said, "will protect the Court."

Black entered the hospital the next morning, August 27. Harlan, undergoing diagnostic testing for recurring back pains, was in the next room.

In contrast to Black, Harlan continued to run his chambers from his hospital bed. Nearly blind, he could not even see the ash from his own cigarette, but he doggedly prepared for the coming term. One day a clerk brought in an emergency petition. Harlan remained in bed as he discussed the case with the clerk. They agreed that the petition should be denied. Harlan bent down, his eyes virtually to the paper, wrote his name, and handed the paper to his clerk. The clerk saw no signature. He looked over at Harlan.

"Justice Harlan, you just denied your sheet," the clerk said gently, pointing to the scrawl on the linen. Harlan smiled and tried again, signing the paper this time.

Black didn't want to see any visitors. He was convinced that he was going to die. Nixon sent a letter saying he wanted to pay him a visit. Black declined. Burger came by to chat but Black didn't respond. Harlan tried repeatedly to cheer Black, and he failed.

"I can't see," Black told one of his sons. "I've got to quit. . . . And I'll tell you something else, John Harlan can't see a thing. He ought to get off the Court, too."*

Black's major concern, from the moment he entered the hospital, was to make sure that his most private papers, memos and conference notes were burned. Publication would inhibit the free exchange of ideas in the future. He felt that he had been treated unfairly in the late Justice Harold H. Burton's diary, in which Burton had written that Black at first resisted desegregation. Black had also been shattered by the biography of former Justice Harlan Fiske Stone, written by Alpheus Thomas Mason. Black had told Burger that when he read Stone's biography, he had discovered for the first time that Stone couldn't stand him.

---

* See Hugo Black, Jr., *My Father: A Remembrance*, p. 249.

Black didn't want that kind of use made of his private papers. He ordered his son, Hugo Jr., to burn them. His son stalled for a time, hoping that his father's condition would improve, but Black's health continued to deteriorate. His papers were finally retrieved and burned. On September 17, Black's messenger delivered his letter of resignation to Nixon. He was 85. He had served 34 terms.

At about the same time, Harlan received the news he had feared. The tests showed that he had cancer. Harlan decided to resign, but he delayed his announcement to avoid detracting from the attention and the adulation he knew Black would receive. On September 23, Harlan submitted his letter of resignation. He was 71 and had served 16 terms.

Two days later, Black died.*

With the Court down to seven justices, the conference met quickly to revise its schedule. The justices realized the Court might be shorthanded for some time if there were protracted confirmation battles.

A number of capital punishment cases, scheduled for argument the first day of the term only two weeks away, were the first to be postponed. Such cases would require a full nine-man court. In any case, Burger was interested in deferring as many cases as

---

* The minister selected to deliver the eulogy went to Black's library and found various books that Black had underlined, including *The Greening of America*, by Charles Reich, one of his former clerks. The minister selected some of the underlined portions to read at the funeral. During the eulogy, Brennan gently nudged Stewart. "Hugo would turn over in his grave if he heard that," Brennan said. Only Black's intimates knew that Black thought Reich's book absurd, and that Black underlined the sections he *disliked*.

possible. Burger was certain that Nixon's new appointees would be natural allies.

But when the administration made its move, it seemed to Burger that Nixon had learned nothing from the Haynsworth-Carswell disasters. The first name that was sent to the American Bar Association screening committee was conservative Republican congressman Richard Poff of Virginia. The prospect was greeted unenthusiastically in legal circles. It seemed unlikely that the ABA committee would give Poff anything approaching a strong endorsement. Poff quickly withdrew his name.

Other possibilities were leaked. One that caused an uproar in the press and legal establishment was Democratic senator Robert Byrd of West Virginia. Nixon wanted Byrd's name sent to the screening committee, even though Byrd, a law school graduate, had never been admitted to the bar and had never practiced law.

From the hospital, Harlan expressed his concern to Stewart about the men being mentioned as possible successors. They were both puzzled by Nixon's seeming willingness to denigrate the Court by once more nominating lackluster, even obviously unacceptable, candidates. The rest of the Court shared Harlan's worry.

Nixon had two criteria. He was still looking for a Southerner, and he wanted another "first" for his administration. He wanted to appoint the first woman to the Court.

Mitchell quickly came up with a male candidate from Arkansas, a local municipal bond lawyer, Herschel Friday. On Thursday afternoon, October 7, Mitchell and Rehnquist interviewed him. The following morning, they interviewed their top woman candidate, Mildred Lillie, a California court of appeals judge.

John Dean, the White House Council since 1970, was sent to interview the candidates. Mitchell had lost some credibility with the president in the wake of the Haynsworth and Carswell failures. Friday was a good lawyer, Dean reported, but he would make Carswell look good as a Senate witness. He knew very little constitutional law and would have trouble being confirmed. Lillie had similar problems, Dean said. The ABA committee probably wouldn't approve her, since she lacked sufficient judicial experience.*

Rehnquist was also unimpressed. "Christ, we've got to be able to do better than this," he told Kleindienst. He preferred New York Court of Appeals Judge Charles D. Breitel, a brilliant conservative jurist.

But Mitchell was satisfied. On Tuesday, October 12, he sent the names of Friday and Lillie to the ABA committee.

Burger was increasingly worried. Another Nixon attempt to appoint someone without qualifications, leading to another drawn-out battle with the Senate, would severely damage the Court's prestige. The possibility that the Court might have to limp along for an entire term with seven justices, because of White House bungling, was intolerable. The chief had discussed the need for prompt and careful selection of candidates with Mitchell on several occasions since Black's and Harlan's resignations. The message didn't seem to be getting through.

On October 13, Burger once more tried to get the point across in a "personal and confidential" letter to Mitchell. Burger asked Mitchell and his "client" (Nixon) to keep the Court's needs in mind. "It is beyond dispute, I think, that the Court as an institution has been sorely damaged in this last decade."

Reminding him of the embarrassment caused by LBJ's effort

---

* See John Dean, *Blind Ambition*, p. 50.

to replace Chief Justice Warren with Fortas, and the subsequent scandal over Fortas's finances, Burger noted that the "completely unwarranted rejection of Judge Haynsworth and the subsequent rejection of Judge Carswell were also bruising episodes.

"The loss in September of two strong and able justices—one of whom had become virtually a legend—is a blow of a different character but, nevertheless, a new injury to the institution," Burger said. The chief said that he understood Nixon's desire to appoint a woman to the Court, but argued against a "woman appointed simply because she is a woman."

Burger also expressed sympathy for Nixon's wish to appoint a Southerner. "As I indicated to you in our conversation some weeks ago and again more recently, I recognize that geographical factors cannot be ignored by the president."

The chief proposed that the president consider two candidates from the South in addition to Herschel Friday, whom he described as an attorney of "very superior professional qualifications." One was Lewis Powell, 64, a private attorney in Richmond and a former president of the ABA. The other was Federal District Judge Frank Johnson of Alabama, a liberal with a strong civil rights record. Burger also put forward the names of seven other judges from the Northeast as possibilities.

The following afternoon, Mitchell and Burger met in the attorney general's office. Two hours later, Mitchell told reporters that the administration was considering nine candidates besides Friday and Lillie.

By Monday, October 18, the head of the screening committee reported that the main candidates, Lillie and Friday, would have serious trouble getting ABA approval. The formal vote would be on Wednesday. Nixon and Mitchell didn't wait. At 8:20 a.m.

Tuesday, Mitchell phoned Lewis Powell at the Waldorf-Astoria Hotel in New York. "I am authorized by the president to offer you an appointment to the Supreme Court," Mitchell said.

Powell declined. He reminded Mitchell of a letter he had written shortly after the Carswell defeat. At the time he had heard that he was on a small list of those under consideration, and he had written Mitchell to say that he didn't want the job, that at 62 he was too old to begin a new career. Now, Powell reminded Mitchell, he was two years older.

Mitchell was aware of the age problem. The president had agreed when Powell's name came up two years earlier that he was too old. He wouldn't have enough time on the Court to really influence it. But now the situation was more urgent. Powell could get confirmed.

Mitchell asked Powell if he would remain by the phone and promised that he would call him back at 10:30 a.m. Powell waited. It was almost 11:15 a.m. when Mitchell called to ask Powell to reconsider. Powell declined again.

Solicitor General Griswold suggested to Mitchell that Powell might react differently to a direct appeal from the president. Powell had barely arrived home in Richmond that night when the phone rang. It was the White House. President Nixon pushed hard. Powell had a "duty" to accept—a duty to the South, to the law, the Court, the president, the country, Nixon said.

Powell told him that he would consider it, but even as he said it, he realized that he couldn't turn down the president.

Powell had been offered Hugo Black's seat. A candidate was still needed for Harlan's. Kleindienst got ready to review the likeliest nominees with Mitchell. Rehnquist, who had participated in most of the meetings, was also preparing for the meeting when

Kleindienst told him to forget it. "We're going to be talking about you," Kleindienst said.

Nixon had certain concerns about nominating Rehnquist. It would look like an "in-house" appointment, and Rehnquist was relatively unknown in establishment legal circles. A former clerk to Justice Robert Jackson in 1952, Rehnquist had practiced law for 16 years in Phoenix where he was part of the Goldwater wing of the Republican Party. He had joined the Justice Department to head the Office of Legal Counsel as an assistant attorney general in 1969. He had been, in effect, Attorney General Mitchell's lawyer.

Nixon had some trouble remembering Rehnquist's name; he once called him "Renchburg." He was also somewhat taken aback by the easygoing lawyer's appearance, once referring to him as "that clown" because of his long sideburns and pink shirts. But Rehnquist was very bright and extremely conservative. And at 47, he could be expected to serve many years.

On Thursday night, October 21, in a televised address, Nixon announced the nominations of Powell and Rehnquist.

———

Nixon thought Powell would be confirmed easily. He was a native Virginian and he had impressive credentials: Phi Beta Kappa from Washington and Lee College in 1929; first in his class at Washington and Lee Law School after completing the three-year course in only two years; a year of graduate work at Harvard Law School; private practice with a prestigious law firm; directorships in 11 major corporations; president of the ABA in 1964–65; president of the American College of Trial Lawyers, 1968–70; and member of Lyndon Johnson's National Crime Commission.

Powell was a political moderate. As vice president of the National Legal Aid & Defender Association, he had played an important role in securing organized bar support for legal services for the poor. As chairman of the Richmond School Board from 1952 to 1961, he kept the Richmond schools open in spite of segregationist pressure to close them in the wake of the *Brown* decisions.

Rehnquist too had excellent credentials: an undergraduate and master's degree from Stanford; a master's in history from Harvard; and editor of the *Law Review* at Stanford Law School.

But Rehnquist might have more trouble than Powell in getting through the Senate. Richard Kleindienst, the deputy attorney general, had brought him to Washington in 1968 to serve as assistant attorney general to advise the department on legal strategy. He had performed brilliantly for the administration—justifying its anticrime measures, its wiretapping of domestic radicals, and the mass arrests during the previous spring's demonstrations. Rehnquist might have done his job too well. He might run into fire from congressional liberals. Black people also seemed certain to oppose his nomination. Rehnquist had testified against a Phoenix civil rights act as recently as 1964, and in favor of limited school desegregation in 1967.

But Nixon had a plan: the two nominations would be sent to the Senate as a package. Powell's supporters worked hard to untie the knot, to try to see that Powell and Rehnquist were not even so much as photographed together in visits to Capitol Hill. Shortly after his nomination, Powell and a group of supporters called on the Senate Judiciary Committee chairman, the conservative James Eastland.

Eastland sat behind his desk, silently puffing his cigar. "You're going to be confirmed," he told Powell.

Powell thanked him.

"Do you know why you're going to be confirmed?" Eastland asked.

No, he replied.

"Because," Eastland drawled, "they think you're going to die."

Eastland was offended by the efforts of Powell's friends to separate his nomination from Rehnquist's. Rehnquist had captured Eastland's affections during his appearances on the Hill. The senator had heard enough from Powell's supporters about how Rehnquist was a lowbrow, not up to the standards of the Supreme Court. To Eastland, that just meant that Rehnquist represented ordinary folk, Middle America. The confirmations, he declared, would be "double or nothing."

Eastland got word that the ABA screening committee was not going to give Rehnquist a favorable recommendation. The committee's authority was only advisory, but an adverse vote might damage Rehnquist's chances by making him seem unqualified. Eastland found that prospect incredible. Rehnquist was no dullard. He had been first in his class at Stanford Law School. There had to be a raw political motive behind this, and Eastland decided to expose it. The chairman passed the word to the ABA committee that if it didn't approve Rehnquist, he would subpoena each of the 12 members to testify about their reasons under oath. Subpoenas were typed; travel plans prepared. Staff members were ready to fan out around the country.

The ABA panel voted on November 2. Powell was unanimously given the highest possible rating. The committee, apparently buckling to Eastland's threat, then voted 9 to 3 to give Rehnquist the highest rating, and even the minority stated that it was "not opposed" to his nomination.

The Senate committee's questioning of Powell in early November was perfunctory. A brief controversy arose over an article that Powell had written for the local Richmond paper four months earlier. The article had attacked the "radical left" and linked it to "foreign Communist enemies." Wiretapping of domestic radicals without obtaining warrants was reasonable and necessary, Powell had written; there was no real distinction between "external and internal threats" to the national security. But the flap over the article was minimal. Powell was confirmed by the Senate on December 6 by a vote of 89 to 1.

Rehnquist received a rougher grilling. His most serious problem arose when a memo surfaced that he had written in the first *Brown* case, when he was clerking for Justice Jackson 19 years earlier. The memo recommended that the Court not order school desegregation. "Separate but equal" facilities were all that was constitutionally required, Rehnquist had stated.

Rehnquist testified that he had written the memorandum, but he denied that it had reflected his views. He was merely summarizing Jackson's views for the conference.

Rehnquist's account was disputed by a lawyer who had clerked with him on the Court, and by Jackson's secretary. Press reports played up the discrepancies in testimony.* But the committee dropped the matter. In two full days of hearings, the liberals could do no more than establish that Rehnquist was every

---

* Douglas, the only remaining member of the Court that had decided the *Brown* cases, examined a copy of Rehnquist's testimony. Rehnquist was correct, he told clerks. The views were, in fact, Jackson's. But see also Richard Kluger, *Simple Justice,* pp. 605–10.

bit as conservative as he appeared to be when defending administration policies. On December 10, the Senate voted to confirm him 68 to 26.

The new justices were to be sworn in after the holidays.

———

Douglas had long wanted the Court to face the abortion issue head-on. The laws in effect in most states, prohibiting or severely restricting the availability of abortions, were infringements of a woman's personal liberty. The broad constitutional guarantee of "liberty," he felt, included the right of a woman to control her body.

Douglas realized, however, that a majority of his colleagues were not likely to give such a sweeping reading to the Constitution on this increasingly volatile issue. He knew also that the two cases now before the Court—challenging restrictive abortion laws in Georgia and Texas *(Doe v. Bolton* and *Roe v. Wade)*—did not signal any sudden willingness on the part of the Court to grapple with the broad question of abortions. They had been taken only to determine whether to expand a series of recent rulings limiting the intervention of federal courts in state court proceedings. Could women and doctors who felt that state prosecutions for abortions violated their constitutional rights, go into federal courts to stop the state? And could they go directly into federal courts even before going through all possible appeals in the state court system? Douglas knew the chief wanted to say no to both these jurisdiction questions. He knew the chief hoped to use these two cases to reduce the number of federal court cases brought by activist attorneys. The two abortion cases were not to be argued primarily about abortion rights, but about jurisdiction. Douglas was doubly discouraged, believing that his side was also going to lose on the jurisdiction issue.

Since Powell and Rehnquist still had not been sworn in, the cases were going to be decided by a seven-man Court. The chief, Stewart, White and Blackmun seemed firmly opposed to taking an expansive view of the range of civil rights cases that could be brought to federal court. So, jurisdiction or abortion, either way it looked like at least a 4-to-3 defeat.

In one case, *Roe v. Wade*, Sarah Weddington, a poised but inexperienced advocate before the Court, argued on behalf of the women hoping to overturn an 1856 Texas law restricting abortions. Unaware the Court was focusing on jurisdiction questions, she immediately began discussing the woman's constitutional right to an abortion.

Stewart pointed out that there were several threshold questions to be dealt with first, including the jurisdiction issue.

Stewart's questions drew Douglas's attention. As always during oral argument, Douglas was a flurry of activity. He listened with one ear, wrote, listened a moment, requested a book from the library, listened again, asked an occasional question, signed his correspondence for the day, listened again, made sarcastic comments to the chief on his left or Stewart on his right. Now, for a change, Douglas stopped dead. He jotted a quick note to his clerks. "I need considerable research" on the jurisdiction question, he wrote. "Would one of you take it on?"

Weddington replied to Stewart that she saw no jurisdiction problem. Under earlier Court decisions, federal courts could intervene in state courts when constitutional issues had been raised. The Court had a number of bases for striking down Texas's abortion law. "We had originally brought the suit alleging both the due process clause, equal protection clause, the Ninth Amendment, and a variety of others," Weddington began. "Since—"

"And anything else that might have been appropriate?" White interjected sarcastically.

"Yes, yeah," Weddington said, dissolving into laughter for a moment. But White had pinned Weddington where he wanted her. She had made a broad constitutional claim, the kind a majority of the Court normally opposed.

"Well, do you or don't you say that the constitutional right you insist on reaches up until the time of birth, or what?" White asked.

". . . The Constitution, as I see it, gives protection to people after birth," she offered.

Douglas then turned the questioning back to the issue they were supposed to be considering, the federal jurisdiction question, and Weddington's time soon lapsed.

When the assistant attorney general of Texas, Jay Floyd, began presenting the state's case, Marshall returned to the issue of abortion. When, he inquired, does an unborn fetus come to have full constitutional rights?

"At any time, Mr. Justice; we make no distinction . . ." Floyd replied. "There is life from the moment of impregnation."

"And do you have any scientific data to support that?" Marshall asked.

"Well, we begin, Mr. Justice, in our brief, with the development of the human embryo, carrying it through to the development of the fetus, from about seven to nine days after conception," Floyd answered.

"Well, what about six days?" Marshall asked, eliciting a mild chuckle from the audience.

"We don't know," Floyd acknowledged.

"But this statute goes all the way back to one hour," Marshall said, clearly enjoying himself.

"I don't—Mr. Justice, it—there are unanswerable questions in this field, I—" Floyd, flustered, was interrupted by laughter around him.

"I appreciate it, I appreciate it," Marshall chanted, leaning back in exaggerated satisfaction with Floyd's befuddlement.

"This is an artless statement on our part," Floyd offered.

"I withdraw the question," Marshall said, trailing off.

Laughter nearly drowned out Floyd as he continued.

The Court turned to the Georgia case, *Doe v. Bolton*. Margie Pitts Hames summarized her client's case against a Georgia law that required abortions to be approved by two doctors and a hospital committee. This case was different from the Texas case, she insisted. There was no question of jurisdiction here, she argued.

Blackmun, energized for the first time that morning, asked questions about why the women who were suing had not sued the hospital as well as the state of Georgia. He also questioned Hames closely on the widespread practice of requiring that medical panels—not simply one doctor—approve certain types of abortion, thus making them difficult to obtain.

Blackmun's tone was hostile throughout. Overall, he had found the quality of oral argument in these cases poor. The abortion issue deserved a better presentation.

The rule of thumb at the Court was that oral arguments rarely win a case, but occasionally lose one. The Texas attorney general would certainly have hurt his case had it not been for the fact that the case would be decided on the question of jurisdiction.

As the father of three outspoken women and the husband of another, Blackmun was sensitive to the abortion issue. Even more, as a former counsel to the Mayo Clinic, he sympathized with the doctor who was interrupted in his medical practice by the state, and told how he could or could not treat his patients. On the other hand, Blackmun generally felt the states should have the right to enforce their legislative will.

———

Stewart thought that abortion was one of those emotional issues that the Court rarely handled well. Yet it was becoming too important to ignore. Abortion was a political issue. Women were coming into their own, as Stewart learned from his daughter, Harriet, a strong, independent woman.

As Stewart saw it, abortion was becoming one reasonable solution to population control. Poor people, in particular, were consistently victims of archaic and artificially complicated laws. The public was ready for abortion reform.

Still, these were issues of the very sort that made Stewart uncomfortable. Precisely because of their political nature, the Court should avoid them. But the state legislatures were always so far behind. Few seemed likely to amend their abortion laws. Much as Stewart disliked the Court's being involved in this kind of controversy, this was perhaps an instance where it had to be involved.

Stewart had no intention, however, of declaring himself the Court's leading activist. The abortion advocates argued that the Court should extend its 1965 decision in a Connecticut birth-control case, *Griswold v. Connecticut.* A majority of the justices had held in that case that, although no right to privacy was explicitly stated in the Constitution, it was implied from a number of the Amendments. They had ruled that Connecticut could not prohibit married couples from using birth-control devices. Abortion advocates wanted that constitutional right to privacy extended to abortion.

Stewart thought that the abortion advocates' argument was too drastic. He had dissented from the 1965 decision, and he was reluctant to renounce his position. It was simply unnecessary for the Court to create another new constitutionally based right.

In a case the previous year *(U.S. v. Vuitch)*, when the Court had upheld restrictions on abortion in the District of Columbia, Douglas had argued in dissent that a physician's judgment on abortion was a professional judgment that should not be second-guessed. Maybe this was the approach.

Stewart thought he could expand Douglas's argument to show that some anti-abortion statutes inhibited a doctor's ability to exercise his best judgment. Since a state-licensed doctor was a professional, the laws should not interfere with his judgment on behalf of his patient. On that theory, Stewart could vote to knock out the Georgia law—which required that abortions be approved by two doctors and a hospital committee—without creating an explicit constitutional right to abortion. But he did not want to be the one to raise this issue in conference.

Douglas had presented this rationale the year before. Since he was the justice most likely to point out any inconsistency by Stewart with his past positions, one of Stewart's clerks went to Douglas's chambers. Stewart was considering voting against the Georgia abortion law, he told one of Douglas's clerks. If Douglas were to resurrect his reasoning, it might help.

The clerks compared notes. It seemed that Blackmun had also asked his clerks to research the same point. Blackmun's high regard for doctors might make him susceptible to this argument. The message from Stewart's clerk was relayed to Douglas.

Douglas was not impressed. Stewart was a patrician, a Rocke-feller Republican; his constituencies were not the poor or women. He was "off in a cloud," hobbled by the *noblesse oblige* of America's upper class. Stewart was more concerned with the appearance of his jurisprudence than with its substance. Douglas was convinced that Stewart was out of touch with three quarters of American society. He used to make fun of Stewart's elitist Yale background. No, Douglas decided, there would be no special assistance for Stewart. As always, Douglas would present his own thoughts and let the others fend for themselves.

The buzzer summoned the seven justices to conference that Thursday. Douglas's travel plans had caused it to be scheduled a day early.

Before dealing with the abortion cases, the conference took up *Mitchum v. Foster*, a case which involved a Florida "adult" book-store that had been shut down by a state judge for peddling ob-scene materials. *Mitchum* posed a similar question of jurisdiction that was presented in the abortion cases. Could the bookstore owner go into federal court before the state courts had finished with the case?

Stewart concluded that, despite restrictions the Court had pre-viously placed on federal-court intervention, the doctrine of non-intervention had its limits. The federal courts must be allowed to intervene wherever a glaring constitutional violation was taking place. Contrary to Douglas's expectation, Stewart joined Douglas, Brennan and Marshall to make it 4 to 3 for asserting federal ju-risdiction.

Since the jurisdiction question here was the same as in the abortion cases, the Court had effectively decided the abortion ju-risdiction issue as well. The Court *did* have jurisdiction. Suddenly, unexpectedly, the Court found itself faced with the underlying constitutional issue in the abortion cases. Did women have a right to obtain abortions?

The chief had some difficulty in summarizing the cases. The Georgia law, requiring approval by two other doctors and then a hospital committee, put unusual restrictions on a physician who wanted to perform an abortion.

As Stewart had hoped, the discussion focused on the professional rights of a doctor seeking to perform an abortion, rather than on the rights of a woman trying to obtain one. Both Stewart and Blackmun were sympathetic to the arguments for lifting some restrictions on physicians. Each justice focused on a different aspect of the case. As discussion continued, their positions emerged:

The chief strongly in favor of upholding the state abortion laws, but not casting a clear vote;

White also for upholding;

Douglas, Brennan and Marshall strongly in favor of striking down the abortion laws on broad grounds of women's constitutional rights;

Stewart and Blackmun in favor of striking down at least portions of some of the laws, if only on narrower grounds of professional discretion.

These are difficult cases, the chief said. No one could really tell how they would come out until the final drafting was done. The cases might even be candidates for reargument after the two new justices were sworn in.

Brennan and Marshall counted the vote 5 to 2—Douglas, Brennan, Marshall, Stewart and Blackmun for striking the laws; the chief and White dissenting.

Douglas, however, thought there were only four votes to strike the laws. Blackmun's vote was far from certain. He could not be counted on to split with the chief on such an important issue.

For his part, Blackmun was for some kind of limited ruling against portions of the law, but he had not decided what to do.

White believed the vote was three for striking—Douglas, Brennan and Marshall; three for upholding—White, Stewart and Blackmun; and the chief, who had passed, but clearly had strong feelings for upholding.

Stewart told his clerks, "We're going to face the abortion issue squarely," and there seemed to him to be a majority to strike the laws. The puzzle was Blackmun.

————

The chief's assignment sheet circulated the following afternoon. Each case was listed on the left side in order of the oral argument, the name of the justice assigned to write each decision on the right.

It took Douglas several moments to grasp the pattern of the assignments, and then he was flabbergasted. The chief had assigned four cases in which Douglas was sure the chief was not a member of the majority. These included the two abortion cases, which the chief had assigned to Blackmun. He could barely control his rage as he ran down the list. Was there some mistake? He asked a clerk to check his notes from the conference. Douglas kept a docket book in which he recorded his tabulation of the votes. It was as he suspected.

In the Florida bookstore case, which raised a similar jurisdictional question as the abortion cases, and in which the chief was a member of the minority, Burger had not only assigned the case but assigned it to another member of the minority. Douglas was all the more incredulous, since this case provided the basis for jurisdiction in the two abortion cases.

In another case *(Gooding v. Wilson)*, the chief had assigned a case in which he and Blackmun were a two-vote minority. Douglas, as the senior justice in the majority, had already assigned this case at conference to Brennan.

In a fifth case *(Alexander v. Louisiana)*, the chief had been in the majority but had assigned Stewart, a member of the minority, to write. Stewart sent the chief a memo declining for that reason.

Never, in Douglas's 33 years on the court, had any chief justice tried to assign from the minority in such fashion. For two terms now there had been incidents when the chief had pleaded ignorance, had claimed he hadn't voted, had changed his vote. Until now they had been isolated instances.

Four misassignments at one time, however, was simply too much to let pass. Douglas was convinced that as the senior member of the majority, he should have assigned all four of the cases. What particularly bothered him was that the chief had given the abortion cases to Blackmun, his personal ally. Blackmun had voted with the chief nearly every time the previous term. The chief might as well have assigned the abortion cases to himself.

On Saturday, December 18, Douglas drafted a scathing memo to Burger, with copies to the other justices. He, not the chief, should have assigned the opinions in four of the cases. And, Douglas added, he would assign the opinions as he saw fit.

The chief's response was back in a day. He conceded error in two of the cases, but insisted that the voting in the two abortion cases was too complicated. "There were . . . literally not enough columns to mark up an accurate reflection of the voting," Burger wrote. "I therefore marked down no votes and said this was a case that would have to stand or fall on the writing, when it was done.

"That is still my view of how to handle these two sensitive cases, which, I might add, are quite probable candidates for reargument."

Douglas ascribed to Burger the most blatant political motives. Nixon favored restrictive abortion laws. Faced with the possibility that the Court might strike abortion laws down in a presidential-election year, the chief wanted to stall the opinion, Douglas concluded.

Blackmun was by far the slowest writer on the Court. The year was nearly half over and he had yet to produce a first circulation in a simple business case that had been argued the first week *(Port of Portland v. U.S.)*. It was the kind of case in which Douglas produced drafts within one week of conference. But in the abortion cases, Douglas had a deeper worry. The chief was trying to manipulate the outcome.

Blackmun might circulate a draft striking portions of the restrictive abortion laws. But as a judicial craftsman, his work was crude. A poor draft would be likely to scare off Stewart, who was already queasy, and leave only four votes. Or if Blackmun himself were to desert the position—a distinct possibility—precious time would be lost. Either defection would leave only a four-man majority. It would be difficult to argue that such a major decision should be handed down on a 4-to-3 vote. There would be increasing pressure to put the cases over for rehearing with the two new Nixon justices. This was no doubt exactly the sort of case that Nixon had in mind when he chose Powell and Rehnquist.

Blackmun was both pleased and frightened by the assignment. It was a no-win proposition. No matter what he wrote, the opinion would be controversial. Abortion was too emotional, the split in society too great. Either way, he would be hated and vilified.

But from Blackmun's point of view, the chief had had little choice but to select him. Burger could not afford to take on such a controversial case himself, particularly from the minority. Douglas was the Court's mischievous liberal, the rebel, and couldn't be the author. Any abortion opinion Douglas wrote would be widely questioned outside the Court, and his extreme views might split rather than unify the existing majority. Lastly, Blackmun had noticed a deterioration in the quality of Douglas's opinions; they had become increasingly superficial.

Brennan was certainly as firm a vote for striking down the state abortion laws as there was on the Court. But Brennan was the Court's only Catholic. As such, Blackmun reasoned, he could not be expected to be willing to take the heat from Catholic anti-abortion groups. Marshall could not be the author for similar reasons: an opinion by the Court's only Black member could be unfairly perceived as specifically designed for Black people. That left only Stewart. Blackmun believed that Stewart would certainly relish the assignment, but he clearly had trouble going very far.

Blackmun was convinced that he alone had the medical background and sufficient patience to sift through the voluminous record for the scientific data on which to base a decision. He was deeply disturbed by Douglas's assumption that the chief had some malicious intent in assigning the abortion cases to him. He was *not* a Minnesota Twin.

True, Blackmun had known the chief since they were small children and had gone to Sunday school together. They had lived four or five blocks apart in the blue-collar Dayton's Bluff section of St. Paul. Neither family had much money during the Depression. The two boys had kept in touch until Blackmun went to a technical high school.

Blackmun's seven years at Harvard, however, put the two men worlds apart. Burger had finished local college and night law school in six years and was already practicing law when Blackmun came back to clerk for a judge on the court of appeals. Blackmun was best man at Burger's wedding, but the two drifted apart again as they established very different law practices.

Blackmun tried to tell his story every chance he got. His hands in his pockets, jingling change uncomfortably, he would explain how he had practiced in Minneapolis, where large law firms concentrated on serving major American corporations. Burger had practiced in St. Paul, across the river, in the political, wheeler-dealer atmosphere of a state capital.

"A Minneapolis firm," Blackmun would say, "will never practice in St. Paul or vice versa." Left unsaid was the disdain so obvious in the Minneapolis legal community for St. Paul lawyers.

But Blackmun was a hesitant and reserved storyteller, and he was never sure that the others got the message. Douglas, however, should have realized by now that Harry Blackmun was no Warren Burger twin.

Blackmun had long thought Burger an uncontrollable, blustery braggart. Now, once again in close contact with him, he was at once put off and amused by the chief's exaggerated pomposity, his callous disregard for the feelings of his colleagues, his self-aggrandizing style. "He's been doing that since he was four," he once told Stewart.

Blackmun was just as aware as Douglas was of the chief's

attempts to use his position to manipulate the Court. Douglas was correct to despise that sort of thing. But this time, Blackmun felt, Douglas was wrong. When he arrived at the Court, Blackmun had assumed the chief's job as scrivener for the conference. Burger had finally given up trying to keep track of all the votes and positions taken in conference, and had asked Blackmun to keep notes and stay behind to brief the clerk of the Court. Even then the chief sometimes misstated the results. Blackmun would deftly field the chief's hesitations, filling in when he faltered. When Burger misinformed the clerk of the Court, Blackmun's cough would cue him.

"Do you recall what happened there, Harry?" the chief would then say. "My notes seem to be a bit sporadic."

Blackmun would fill in the correct information as if Burger had initiated the request.

Part of the problem was that the chief spread himself too thin. He accepted too many social, speaking and ceremonial engagements, and exhibited too little affection for the monastic, scholarly side of the Court's life. As a result, Burger was often unprepared for orals or conference. Too often, he had to wait and listen in order to figure out which issues were crucial to the outcome. His grasp of the cases came from the summaries, usually a page or less, of the cert memos his clerks prepared. The chief rarely read the briefs or the record before oral argument.

The problem was compounded by Burger's willingness to change his position in conference, or his unwillingness to commit himself before he had figured out which side had a majority. Then, joining the majority, he could control the assignment. Burger had strained his relationship with everyone at the table to the breaking point. It was as offensive to Blackmun as it was to the others. But one had to understand the chief. For all his faults, here was a self-made man who had come up the ladder rung by rung. Blackmun did not begrudge him his attempts at leadership.

The abortion assignment really amounted to nothing more than a request that Blackmun take first crack at organizing the issues. It was one of those times when the conference had floundered, when the briefs and oral arguments had been inadequate, when the seemingly decisive issue in the case, jurisdiction, had evaporated. The Court had been left holding the bull by the tail.

Blackmun was not so naïve as to think that the chief had given him the abortion cases with the intention of having him find a broad constitutional right to abortion. But he was distressed by Douglas's implicit suggestion that he was unfit for the assignment or was somehow involved in a deception.

Blackmun also knew that he, after all, had a unique appreciation of the problems and strengths of the medical profession. At Mayo, he had watched as Drs. Edward C. Kendall and Philip S. Hench won the Nobel Prize for research in arthritis. He rejoiced with other doctors after their first successful heart-bypass operation, then suffered with them after they lost their next four patients. He sat up late nights with the surgical staff to review hospital deaths in biweekly meetings, and recalled them in detail. He grew to respect what dedicated physicians could accomplish. These had been terribly exciting years for Blackmun. He called them the best 10 years of his life.

If a state licensed a physician to practice medicine, it was entrusting him with the right to make medical decisions. State laws restricting abortions interfered with those medical judgments. Physicians were always somewhat unsure about the possible legal ramifications of their judgments. To completely restrict an operation like abortion, normally no more dangerous than minor surgery, or to permit it only with the approval of a hospital committee or the concurrence of other doctors, was a needless infringement of the discretion of the medical profession.

Blackmun would do anything he could to reduce the anxiety of his colleagues except to spurn the assignment. The case was not so much a legal task as an opportunity for the Court to ratify the best possible medical opinion. He would take the first crack at the abortion cases. At the least, he could prepare a memo to clarify the issues.

———

As was his custom, Douglas rushed through a first draft on the cases five days after conference. He decided not to circulate it, but to sit back and wait for Blackmun. He was still bitter toward Burger, whom he had taken to calling "this chief," reserving "The chief" as an accolade fitting only for retired Chief Justice Earl Warren. But Douglas broke his usual rule against lobbying and paid a visit to Blackmun. Though he would have much preferred that Brennan write the draft, he told Blackmun, "Harry, I would have assigned the opinion to you anyway."

Reassured, Blackmun withdrew to his regular hideaway, the justices' second-floor library, where he worked through the winter and spring, initially without even a law clerk to help with research.

Brennan too had little choice but to wait for Blackmun's draft. But in the interval, he spotted a case that he felt might help Blackmun develop a constitutional grounding for a right to abortion. Brennan was writing a majority opinion overturning birth-control activist Bill Baird's conviction for distributing birth-control devices without a license (*Eisenstadt v. Baird*). He wanted to use the case to extend to individuals the right to privacy that was given to married couples by the 1965 Connecticut birth-control case.

Brennan was aware that he was unlikely to get agreement on such a sweeping extension. He circulated his opinion with a carefully worded paragraph at the end. "If the right to privacy means anything, it is the right of the individual, married or single, to be free from unwarranted government intrusion into matters so fundamentally affecting a person as the decision whether to bear or beget a child."

That case dealt only with contraception—the decision to "beget" a child. He included the reference to the decision to "bear" a child with the abortion cases in mind. Brennan hoped the language would help establish a constitutional basis, under the right to privacy, for a woman's right to abortion.

Since the last paragraph was not the basis for the decision, Stewart could join it without renouncing his dissent in the 1965 case. Brennan got Stewart's vote.

But Blackmun was holding back. The chief was lobbying Blackmun not to join Brennan's draft. Brennan's clerks urged their boss to lobby Blackmun.

Brennan refused. Blackmun reminded him, he said, of former justice Charles E. Whittaker, who had been paralyzed by indecisiveness. Whittaker's indecision had ended in a nervous breakdown and his resignation. Former justice Felix Frankfurter had misunderstood Whittaker's indecision and had spent hours lobbying him. Instead of influencing him, Frankfurter had drawn Whittaker's resentment. No, Brennan said, he would not lobby Blackmun.

Blackmun finally decided not to join Brennan's opinion, but simply to concur in the result. That worried Brennan. Without adopting some logic similar to that provided in the contraception case, Blackmun would have difficulty establishing a right to abortion on grounds of privacy.

———

With the official arrival of Powell and Rehnquist, the chief scheduled a January conference to discuss which cases should be put over for reargument before the new nine-man Court. Burger suggested that cases with a 4-to-3 vote should be reargued. His list included the abortion cases, as well as the Florida adult-bookstore case that had settled the question of federal jurisdiction.

Douglas, Brennan, Marshall and Stewart objected vigorously. The Court had an obligation to dispose of every case it could, Douglas argued, leaving the second half of the term free for important cases they had still to deal with, including the death penalty.

The chief was equally determined. The 4-to-3 cases, particularly those in which two new conservative members might likely change the outcome, should be put over. As always, the majority would determine what cases to put over, but Burger argued that the new justices should be allowed to vote on whether these cases should be reargued.

That was impossible, Douglas insisted. The new justices could not vote. Their votes could determine the outcome of the very cases being debated. The internal operating rules, though they were unwritten, must be inviolable.

White said it was important that the Court not discredit itself by deciding cases one way and then shifting and deciding them the other way. Two votes added to the minority side of a 4 to 3 would become a new 5-to-4 majority. The others stirred uncomfortably in their seats. They were unsure of their ground and no one wanted to force the issue.

Powell and Rehnquist said they would prefer not to participate in any vote on whether to hold the cases over for reargument. It was up to the other seven. Powell added that he wasn't sure how he would come out on the cases, particularly the abortion cases. They should not be reargued for him.

One 4-to-3 case involved an antiwar demonstrator who had cursed at a policeman *(Gooding v. Wilson)*. The chief said it should be reargued.

Douglas was sure the vote had been 5 to 2. "Who was the third vote to reverse?" he asked.

"White," the chief replied.

His jaw jutting out, White stared at the chief. No, he was with the majority, he stated. The issue of reargument was finally dropped.

Brennan was relieved. In fact, they didn't even have a draft in the abortion cases. Maybe they were getting ahead of themselves. If Blackmun and Stewart shifted positions, then he, Douglas and Marshall might be on the short end of a 4 to 3, themselves demanding that the abortion cases be put over.

———

Blackmun spent his time—apart from oral argument, conferences and a bare minimum of office routine—in the justices' library. Awesome quantities of medical, as well as legal, books were regularly carried in. But all indications pointed toward no circulation of a first draft until much later in the spring.

Burger had not yet given up on the federal jurisdiction issue. If he could derail the opinion on this important subject, the abortion issue would not have to be decided. On January 25, 1972, the chief circulated a memo and a historical analysis raising three problems with the federal jurisdiction issue settled in the Florida bookstore case that Douglas had assigned to Stewart.

Stewart was not yet prepared to respond. Instead of circulating his opinion, he circulated a memo that Harlan had prepared over the summer on the history of the issue.

Douglas then had one of his clerks get out an elaborate memo on the issue. Unusually detailed and well documented, it responded to each of the questions the chief had raised. The four-member majority on jurisdiction held firm.

Blackmun began each day by breakfasting with his clerks in the Court's public cafeteria, and clerks from the other chambers had a standing invitation to join them. Blackmun would often spot a clerk from another chamber eating alone and invite him over. He seemed, at first, the most open, unassuming and gracious of the justices.

Breakfast-table conversation generally began with sports, usually baseball, and then moved on to the morning's headlines. There was an unspoken rule that any discussion of cases was off limits. Where other justices might openly debate cases with the clerks, Blackmun awkwardly sidestepped each attempt. The law in general was similarly out of bounds. Blackmun turned the most philosophical of discussions about law around to his own experience, or to the clerk's family, or the performance of a younger sibling in school.

The clerks in his own chambers saw a different side of Blackmun which betrayed more of the pressure that he felt. The stories were petty. An office window left open all night might set him off on a tirade. It was not the security that worried Blackmun, but the broken social contract—all clerks were supposed to close all windows each night. Number-two pencils, needle-sharp, neatly displayed in the pencil holder, need include only one number three or a cracked point to elicit a harsh word. If Blackmun wanted a document photocopied, and somehow the wrong one came back, he might simply fling it aside. An interruption, even for some important question, might be repulsed testily.

The mystery of the Blackmun personality deepened. His outbursts varied in intensity and usually passed quickly. "Impatient moods," his secretary called them. But they made life more difficult; they added an extra tension.

Yet none of his Court family—clerks, secretaries or his messenger—judged Blackmun harshly. They all knew well enough the extraordinary pressures, real and imagined, that he worked under.

From his first day at the Court, Blackmun had felt unworthy, unqualified, unable to perform up to standard. He felt he could equal the chief and Marshall, but not the others. He became increasingly withdrawn and professorial. He did not enjoy charting new paths for the law. He was still learning. The issues were too grave, the information too sparse. Each new question was barely answered, even tentatively, when two more questions appeared on the horizon. Blackmun knew that his colleagues were concerned about what they perceived as his indecisiveness. But what others saw as an inability to make decisions, he felt to be a deliberate withholding of final judgment until all the facts were in, all the arguments marshaled, analyzed, documented.

It was a horribly lonely task. Blackmun worked by himself, beginning with a long memo from one of his clerks, reading each of the major briefs, carefully digesting each of the major opinions that circulated, laboriously drafting his own opinions, checking each citation himself, refining his work through a dozen drafts to take into account each justice's observations. He was unwilling, moreover, to debate the basic issues in a case, even in chambers with his own clerks. He preferred that they write him memos.

Wearing a gray or blue cardigan sweater, Blackmun hid away in the recesses of the justices' library, and his office had instructions not to disturb him there. The phone did not ring there, and not even the chief violated his solitude. Working at a long mahogany table lined on the opposite edge with a double row of books, Blackmun took meticulous notes. He spent most of his time sorting facts and fitting them to the law in a desperate attempt to discover inevitable conclusions. He tried to reduce his risks by mastering every detail, as if the case were some huge math problem. Blackmun felt that if all the steps were taken, there could be only one answer.

These abortion cases were his greatest challenge since he came to the Court. Beyond the normal desire to produce an opinion that would win the respect of his peers in the legal community, Blackmun also wanted an opinion that the medical community would accept, one that would free physicians to exercise their professional judgment.

As general counsel at the Mayo Clinic, Blackmun had advised the staff on the legality of abortions the hospital had performed. Many of them would not have qualified under the Texas and Georgia laws now in question.

Blackmun plowed through both common law and the history of English and American law on the subject. He was surprised to find that abortion had been commonly accepted for thousands of years, and that only in the nineteenth century had it become a crime in the United States. At that time, abortion had been a very risky operation, often fatal. The criminal laws had been enacted largely to protect pregnant women.

The use of antiseptics and the availability of antibiotics now made abortion relatively safe, particularly in the first few months of pregnancy. The mortality rates for women undergoing early abortions were presently lower than the mortality rates for women with normal childbirths. That medical reality was central for Blackmun. It was itself a strong medical justification for permitting early abortions.

A decision to abort was one that Blackmun hoped he would never face in his own family. He presumed that his three daughters felt that early abortions should be allowed. He claimed to be unsure of his wife, Dottie's, position. But she told one of his clerks, who favored lifting the restrictions, that she was doing everything she could to encourage her husband in that direction. "You and I are working on the same thing," she said. "Me at home and you at work."

By mid-May, after five months of work, Blackmun was still laboring over his memorandum. Finally, he let one of his clerks look over a draft. As usual, he made it clear that he did not want any editing. The clerk was astonished. It was crudely written and poorly organized. It did not settle on any analytical framework, nor did it explain on what basis Blackmun had arrived at the apparent conclusion that women had a right to privacy, and thus a right to abortion. Blackmun had avoided extending the right of privacy, or stating that the right to abortion stemmed from that right. He seemed to be saying that a woman could get an abortion in the early period of pregnancy. The reason, however, was lost in a convoluted discussion of the "viability of the fetus," the point at which the fetus could live outside the womb. Blackmun had added the general notion that as the length of the pregnancy increased, the states' interest in regulating or prohibiting abortions also increased. But there was no real guidance from which conclusions could be drawn. Blackmun had simply asserted that the Texas law was vague and thus unconstitutional.

The clerk realized that the opinion could not settle any constitutional question. It did not assert, or even imply, that abortion restrictions in the early months of pregnancy were unconstitutional. The result of this opinion would be that restrictive laws, if properly defined by the states, could be constitutional.

The draft seemed to fly in the face of Blackmun's statements to his clerks. "We want to definitely solve this," he had told them. But he seemed to be avoiding a solution.

In the Georgia case, he had found that the law infringed on a doctor's professional judgment, his right to give advice to his patients. Blackmun proceeded from the doctor's point of view; a woman's right to seek and receive medical advice did not seem an issue.

Blackmun's clerk, who favored an opinion that would establish a woman's constitutional right to abortion, began the laborious task of trying to rehabilitate the draft. But Blackmun resisted any modification of his basic reasoning or his conclusions. He circulated the memo to all chambers with few changes.

Stewart was disturbed by the draft. Aside from its inelegant construction and language, it seemed to create a *new* affirmative constitutional right to abortion that was not rooted in any part of the Constitution. Stewart had been expecting a majority opinion. Blackmun's memo did not even have the tone of an opinion, merely of a tentative discussion.

Stewart decided to write his own concurrence, specifying that family-planning decisions, including early abortions, were among the rights encompassed by the Ninth Amendment, which says that the people retain other, unspecified rights beyond those enumerated in the Constitution. Rather than identify the rights that women or doctors have, Stewart preferred to say that states could not properly interfere in individuals' decisions to have early abortions. He circulated his memo two weeks after Blackmun's but immediately joined Blackmun's original.

Douglas saw no shortage of problems with the Blackmun draft, but Blackmun had come a long way. At least it was a step in the right direction. Though Douglas was still holding on to his concurrence, he did not circulate it. Instead, he joined Blackmun.

At the time, the Court was considering an antitrust case against a utility company, the Otter Tail Power Company, which operated in Minnesota. Douglas saw an opportunity to flatter Blackmun. "Harry, you're not a Minnesota Twin with the chief," he told him. "I am the real Minnesota Twin. . . . We were both born in Minnesota and you were not."

Blackmun appreciated the point.

"Furthermore, Harry, I belong to the Otter Tail County regulars. You can't belong, because you weren't born there."

Douglas regaled Blackmun with stories of his father's life as an itinerant preacher in Otter Tail County, and he praised Blackmun's abortion draft. It was one of the finest presentations of an issue he had ever seen, he said.

Blackmun was ecstatic. Douglas, the greatest living jurist, had freed him of the stigma of being Burger's double. Soon, Blackmun had five votes—his own and those of Douglas, Brennan, Marshall and Stewart. It was one more than he needed; it would have been a majority even if Powell and Rehnquist had participated.

For White the term had its ups and downs like any other year at the Court. He had been a fierce competitor all his life. He loved to take control of a case, pick out the weaknesses in the other justices' positions, and then watch them react to his own twists and turns as he pushed his own point of view. When he could not, which was often, he took his frustrations to the fourth-floor gym to play in the clerks' regular full-court basketball game.

Muscling out men 30 years his junior under the boards, White delighted in playing a more competitive game than they did. He dominated the games by alternating savage and effective drives to the basket with accurate two-hand push shots from 20 feet. White consistently pushed off the clerk trying to cover him, calling every conceivable foul against the hapless clerk, while bitching about every foul called against himself. He regularly took the impermissible third step before shooting. The game was serious business for White. Each man was on his own. Teamwork was valuable in order to win, not for its own sake.

One Friday afternoon White was out of position for a rebound, but he went up throwing a hip. A clerk pulled in the ball and White came crashing down off balance and injured his ankle.

The justice came to the office on crutches the next Monday: he would be off the basketball court for the rest of the season. He asked the clerks to keep the reason for his injury secret. The clerks bought him a Fussball game, a modern version of the ancient game of skittles. It was competition, so White enjoyed it, but it lacked for him the thrill of a contact sport like basketball—or law.

On Friday, May 26, White read a draft dissent to Blackmun's abortion decision that one of his clerks had prepared. He then remolded it to his liking. The structure of Blackmun's opinion was juvenile; striking the Texas law for vagueness was simply stupid. The law might have several defects, but vagueness was not among them. The law could not be more specific in delineating the circumstance when abortion was available—it was only to protect the life of the mother.

Blackmun was disturbed by White's attack, but whether it made sense or not, it showed him that he had more work to do. The more he studied and agonized over his own memo, the less pleased he was. He needed more information, more facts, more insight. What was the history of the proscription in the Hippocratic oath which forbade doctors from performing abortions? What was the medical state of the art of sustaining a fetus outside the womb? When did life really begin? When was a fetus fully viable? What were the positions of the American Medical Association, the American Psychiatric Association, the American Public Health Association?

These and dozens of other questions plagued Blackmun. His opinion needed to be stronger. It needed more votes, which could mean wider public acceptance. A nine-man court was essential to bring down such a controversial opinion. "I think we can get Powell," he told his clerks.

One Saturday toward the end of May, the chief paid Blackmun a visit, leaving his armed chauffeur-bodyguard in the outer office. Blackmun's clerks waited anxiously for hours to find out what case the chief was lobbying. The chief finally left, but Blackmun also departed without a word to his clerks. The next week, the chief shifted sides to provide the crucial fifth vote for Blackmun's majority in an antitrust case against professional baseball *(Flood v. Kuhn)*.

The following Saturday, June 3, Blackmun drafted a memorandum withdrawing his abortion opinion. It was already late in the term, he wrote. Such a sensitive case required more research, more consideration. It would take him some time both to accommodate the suggestions of those in the majority, and to respond to the dissenters. Perhaps it would be best if the cases were reargued in the fall. He asked that all copies of his draft memo be returned.

Douglas was once again enraged. The end of the year always involved a crunch. Of course, there was tremendous pressure to put out major opinions without the time to fully refine them. That was the nature of their work. The pressure affected them all. It was typical that Blackmun could not make up his mind and let his opinion go. Douglas had heard that the chief had been lobbying Blackmun. This time, Burger had gone too far. The opinion had five firm votes. It ought to come down. It was not like cases with only four votes that might change when Powell's and Rehnquist's votes were added. Douglas also did not want to give the chief the summer to sway Blackmun.

Burger was taking the position that there were now five votes to put the case over to the next term—Blackmun, White, Powell, Rehnquist and himself. Douglas couldn't believe it. Burger and White were in the minority; they should have no say in what the majority did. And Powell and Rehnquist had not taken part; obviously they could not vote on whether the case should be put over.

The looming confrontation worried Blackmun. There were

no written rules on such questions, and Douglas's apparent willingness to push to a showdown would further inflame the issue. Finally, Blackmun turned to Brennan, who was sympathetic. Obviously the opinion could not come down if its author did not want it to come down. But Brennan also wanted it out as soon as possible.

Blackmun said he understood that Douglas did not trust him, but insisted that he was firm for striking down the abortion law. The vote would go the same way the next year. They might even pick up Powell. That would make the result more acceptable to the public. He would be able to draft a better opinion over the summer.

Brennan was not so certain of Blackmun's firmness. At the same time, he did not want to alienate him. He agreed to tell Douglas that he too was going to vote to put the case over for reargument. He was fairly certain Marshall and Stewart would join. That would leave Douglas protesting alone.

Douglas was not pleased by the news of Brennan's defection. But the battle was not yet over. He dashed off a memo, rushed it to the secretaries for typing and to the printers for a first draft. This time, Douglas threatened to play his ace. If the conference insisted on putting the cases over for reargument, he would dissent from such an order, and he would publish the full text of his dissent. Douglas reiterated the protest he had made in December about the chief's assigning the case to Blackmun, Burger's response and his subsequent intransigence. The senior member of the majority should have assigned the case, Douglas said, and continued:

When, however, the minority seeks to control the assignment, there is a destructive force at work in the Court.

When a Chief Justice tries to bend the Court to his will by manipulating assignments, the integrity of the institution is imperilled.

Historically, this institution has been composed of fiercely independent men with fiercely opposed views. There have been—and will always be—clashes of views. But up to now the Conference, though deeply disagreeing on legal and constitutional issues, has been a group marked by good-will. Up until now a majority view, no matter how unacceptable to the minority, has been honored as such. And up until now the incumbents have honored and revered the institution more than their own view of the public good.

Perhaps the purpose of THE CHIEF JUSTICE, a member of the minority in the *Abortion Cases*, in assigning the opinions was to try to keep control of the merits. If that was the aim, he was unsuccessful. Opinions in these two cases have been circulated and each commands the votes of five members of the Court. Those votes are firm, the Justices having spent many, many hours since last October mulling over every detail of the cases. The cases should therefore be announced.

The plea that the cases be reargued is merely strategy by a minority somehow to suppress the majority view with the hope that exigencies of time will change the result. That might be achieved of course by death or conceivably retirement.

Douglas knew a fifth Nixon appointment was a real possibility on a Court with a 74-year-old man with a pacemaker; with

Marshall, who was chronically ill; and with Brennan, who occasionally threatened to quit.

> But that kind of strategy dilutes the integrity of the Court and makes the decisions here depend on the manipulative skills of a Chief Justice.
>
> The *Abortion Cases* are symptomatic. This is an election year. Both political parties have made abortion an issue. What the parties say or do is none of our business. We sit here not to make the path of any candidate easier or more difficult. We decide questions only on their constitutional merits. To prolong these *Abortion Cases* into the next election would in the eyes of many be a political gesture unworthy of the Court.
>
> Each of us is sovereign in his own right. Each arrived on his own. Each is beholden to no one.

Borrowing a line from a speech he had given in September in Portland, Douglas then made it clear that, despite what he had said earlier, he did in fact view the chief and Blackmun as Nixon's Minnesota Twins. "Russia once gave its chief justice two votes; but that was too strong even for the Russians. . . .

"I dissent with the deepest regret that we are allowing the consensus of the Court to be frustrated."

Douglas refined his draft three times, circulated it, and left for his summer retreat, Goose Prairie.

The Court erupted in debate over whether Douglas was bluffing or was really willing to publish the document. Though sympathetic to his views, Brennan, Marshall and Stewart could not believe that Douglas would go through with it. No one in

the history of the Court had published such a dissent. The chief
might be a scoundrel, but making public the Court's inner mach-
inations was a form of treason. And the reference to the Rus-
sian chief justice with two votes was particularly rough. They
pleaded with Douglas to reconsider. His dissent would undermine the Court's credibility, the principal source of its power.
Its strength derived from the public belief that the Court was
trustworthy, a nonpolitical deliberative body. Did he intend to
undermine all that?

Douglas insisted. He would publish what he felt like publishing. And he would publish this if the request to put over the abortion decision was not withdrawn.

But, the others argued, what good would it do to drag their
internal problems into public view?

It would have a sobering influence on Blackmun, Douglas re-
torted. It would make it harder for him to change his mind over
the summer.

Brennan's impatience with Douglas turned to anger. Douglas
had become an intellectually lazy, petulant, prodigal child. He
was not providing leadership. Douglas was never around when he
was needed. His departure for Goose Prairie was typical. He was
not even, for that matter, pulling his share of the load, though he
certainly contributed more than his share to the tension. The ulti-
mate source of conflict was the chief. But Douglas too was at fault.

Finally, Brennan gave up arguing.

Blackmun then took it up, pleading with Douglas to reconsider. He insisted that he was committed to his opinion. He would
bring it down the same way the next term; more research would
perhaps pick up another vote.

Douglas was unconvinced. He needed time to think it over. His clerks would remain instructed to publish the opinion if the cases were put over for reargument.

But Blackmun had made his point. Douglas finally decided that he couldn't publish. It would endanger next term's vote on the abortion cases.

No longer speaking to his own clerks, whom he blamed for slow mail delivery to Goose Prairie, Douglas called Brennan and told him to have his dissent held. A memo came around to the justices from Douglas's chamber asking for all the copies back.

The conference agreed to put over the abortion cases, but they would not announce their decision until the final day of the term.

1972 TERM

HARRY BLACKMUN RETURNED TO ROCHESTER, Minnesota, for the summer of 1972 and immersed himself in research at the huge Mayo Clinic medical library. Rochester and the clinic were home to Blackmun, a safe harbor after a stormy term. He worked in a corner of the assistant librarian's office for two weeks without saying a word to anyone on the Mayo staff about the nature of his inquiry.

In his summer office in a Rochester high-rise, Blackmun began to organize the research that would bolster his abortion opinion. He talked by phone nearly every day with one of his clerks who had agreed to stay in Washington for the summer.

Blackmun pondered the relevance of the Hippocratic oath, which prohibits doctors from performing abortions. He also wanted to understand the positions of the medical organizations and to learn more about the advances in sustaining the life of a fetus outside the womb.

One by one, new elements found their way into his draft. His clerk worked each change into the text back in Washington. The language remained Blackmun's; the more rigorous analysis was the work of the clerk. For the first time, the right to privacy emerged explicitly. It was not absolute. It was limited by the state's interest in protecting the pregnant woman's health and the potential life of the fetus.

As they developed their analytic basis, Blackmun and his clerk tried to answer the crucial question: when did the state's interest in protecting the life of the fetus become overriding and outweigh the woman's right to privacy? Clearly there was such a point. The state's interest increased with time. But no definite answer could be derived from the Constitution.

Blackmun turned to medicine. Doctors often divided pregnancies into three equal stages, or trimesters, each of roughly three months. Abortions were generally safe in the first trimester and, under proper medical conditions, could be performed safely in the second. It was at about this time, at the end of the second trimester, that the fetus became *viable*, or capable of living outside the womb. That was at about 24 to 28 weeks, six months for all practical purposes. Therefore, the two medical interests—protecting both the health of the mother and the potential life of the fetus—seemed to converge and become overriding at about this six-month point. Abortions during the first two trimesters could and should be permitted. The draft gradually emerged as a strong, liberal prescription. It would prohibit states from interfering until the third trimester.

The clerk who was working on the opinion began to worry that one of the other clerks, strongly opposed to abortions, might try to change their boss's mind. He took no chances. Each night he carefully locked up the work he had been doing for Blackmun. At the end of the summer, he carefully sealed the latest draft in an envelope, put his initials across the tape, and had it locked in Blackmun's desk. Only Blackmun's personal secretary knew where it was.

Powell also made abortion his summer research project. As a young lawyer in Richmond in the 1930s, Powell had heard tales of girls who would "go away" to Switzerland and New York, where safe abortions were available. If someone were willing to pay for it, it was possible to have an abortion.

Powell understood how doctors viewed abortion. His father-in-law had been a leading obstetrician in Richmond, and his two brothers-in-law were obstetricians. Powell had heard all the horrifying stories of unsanitary butchers and coat-hanger abortions.

Nevertheless, Powell came quickly to the conclusion that the Constitution did not provide meaningful guidance. The right to privacy was tenuous; at best it was implied. If there was no way to find an answer in the Constitution, Powell felt he would just have to vote his "gut." He had been critical of justices for doing exactly that; but in abortion, there seemed no choice.

When he returned to Washington, he took one of his law clerks to lunch at the Monocle Restaurant on Capitol Hill. The abortion laws, Powell confided, were "atrocious." His would be a strong and unshakable vote to strike them. He needed only a rationale for his vote.

In a recent lower court case, a federal judge had struck down the Connecticut abortion law.* This opinion impressed Powell. The judge had said that moral positions on abortion "about which each side was so sure must remain a personal judgment, one that [people] may follow in their personal lives and seek to persuade

---

* *Abele v. Markle.*

others to follow, but a judgment they may not impose upon others by force of law." That was all the rationale Powell needed.

———————

Brennan and Douglas worried that votes might have shifted since the previous spring. Blackmun remained a question mark, Stewart might defect, and they were not sure what Powell would do.

At conference on October 12, Blackmun made a long, eloquent and strongly emotional case for striking down the laws. Stewart too seemed ready to join. But the big surprise was Powell. He made it 6 to 3.

Immediately after conference, Douglas called Blackmun to tell him that his presentation had been the finest he had heard at conference in more than 30 years. He hoped the call would sustain Blackmun for the duration.

Before the end of October, Blackmun's new draft in the abortion cases was circulated to the various chambers.

Brennan read it carefully. He waded through the positions of the medical professional organizations, the expanded historical section, the long-winded digest of the medical state of the art. Despite all this, Blackmun's bottom line was acceptable. The states would be prohibited from regulating abortions until "viability." That meant state regulation only during the third trimester. But Brennan spotted a weakness in the argument. Connecting the state's interest in the fetus to the point of viability was risky. Blackmun himself had noted that medical advances made fetuses viable increasingly early. Scientists might one day be capable of sustaining a two-week-old fetus outside the womb. Advances in medicine could undermine the thrust of the opinion.

Brennan had other concerns. Blackmun had focused on the

rights of the doctor and the rights of the state. The most important party, the woman, had been largely neglected. Her rights were
the ones that needed to be upheld.

Brennan found yet another analytical fault in the draft. Blackmun had discussed at length the state's dual interests in protecting the pregnant woman's health and the potential life of the
fetus. Both interests were closely intertwined in Blackmun's draft.
Brennan thought they were quite distinct. He handed Blackmun's
draft to one of his clerks. "It doesn't do it," he said.

Brennan's clerks worked up a long memorandum. The delicate
question, however, was how to communicate Brennan's thoughts
to Blackmun. If Brennan phoned and said, "Harry, here are my
ideas," Blackmun might be intimidated or fumble for months and
still not change the draft adequately. On the other hand, if Brennan sent a printed opinion to the conference, Blackmun might
think he was trying to steal the majority. The last thing Brennan wanted was to author the Court's abortion decision. He could
imagine too vividly what the Catholic bishops would say.

In mid-November, Brennan took his clerks' memo and recast
it as a series of casual thoughts and suggestions. It was important
that it not appear to be an alternative draft. Brennan addressed a
cover memo to Blackmun saying he fully agreed with his draft,
but wanted to pass along some ideas. Brennan's thoughts ran 48
pages. Copies were sent to all the justices.

Blackmun liked some of Brennan's suggestions. He quickly
sent a memo to the justices saying that he was incorporating them.
Before he revised his draft, however, he decided that there was another set of views to be taken into account.

The chief had made it clear to Blackmun that he would "never"
join the draft as it stood, permitting unrestricted abortions up to

viability, or the end of the second trimester. Blackmun wanted the chief's vote, and he thought he saw a way to get it while still taking into account Brennan's suggestions. Instead of the one demarcation line, viability, Blackmun would create two. This would also be more medically sophisticated; it would show that the two state interests—protecting the pregnant woman's health and protecting potential life of the fetus—arose at different times. He settled on a formula.

1. First 12 weeks (first trimester); no state interest at all; abortions unrestricted and left up to the medical judgment of the doctor.

2. 13 to 24 weeks (second trimester); state interest arises and abortions can be regulated only to protect the woman's health.

3. After 24 weeks (third trimester); state interest arises to protect the potential life of the fetus.

This formula had the effect of somewhat limiting abortions in the second trimester. But eliminating viability as the dividing point, Brennan's worry, guaranteed that medical science could not keep reducing the time period during which abortions would be legally available.

Marshall was not happy with Blackmun's proposal. It was too rigid. Many women, particularly the poor and undereducated, would probably not get in touch with a doctor until sometime after the first 12 weeks. A woman in a rural town might not have access to a doctor until later in pregnancy. And according to the Blackmun proposal, the states could effectively ban abortions in the 13-to-24-week period under the guise of protecting the woman's health. Marshall preferred Blackmun's original linkage to viability. If viability were the cutoff point, it would better protect the rural poor. Clearly, viability meant one thing in Boston, where there were fancy doctors and hospitals. There, a fetus might be sustained after only a few months. But in rural areas with no hospitals and few, if any, doctors, viability was probably close to full-term, or late in the third trimester.

Marshall presented all this to Blackmun in a memo.

Blackmun respected Marshall's point of view. Marshall clearly knew a lot about many real-world problems that Blackmun would never see. He incorporated all of Marshall's suggestions. His new draft specified:

1. For the stage up to "approximately" the end of the first trimester, abortions would be left to the medical judgment of the doctor.

2. For the stage after "approximately" the end of the first trimester, abortion procedures could be regulated to protect the woman's health.

3. For the stage after "viability," abortions could be regulated or even prohibited, to protect the fetus.

The clerks in most chambers were surprised to see the justices, particularly Blackmun, so openly brokering their decision like a group of legislators. There was a certain reasonableness to the draft, some of them thought, but it derived more from medical and social policy than from constitutional law. There was something embarrassing and dishonest about this whole process. It left the Court claiming that the Constitution drew certain lines at trimesters and viability. The Court was going to make a medical policy and force it on the states. As a practical matter, it was not a bad solution. As a constitutional matter, it was absurd. The draft was referred to by some clerks as "Harry's abortion."

Stewart had one more change that he insisted on before he would join the opinion. It was imperative that they say more clearly that a fetus was not—as far as the Fourteenth Amendment was concerned—a person. If the fetus were a person, it had rights protected by the Constitution, including "life, liberty and property." Then the Court would be saying that a woman's rights outweighed those of the fetus. Weighing two sets of rights would be dangerous. The Court would be far better off with only one set of rights to protect. Stewart was certain that in legal terms a fetus was not a person. No previous case had held so. States conceded that, where the mother's life was at stake, a fetus had no rights. When the Fourteenth Amendment was passed in 1868, abortions were common enough to suggest that the state legislatures that had ratified the Amendment did not consider fetuses to have rights.

Blackmun did not disagree, but he felt the point was implicit in the opinion. Why expand it and stir up trouble?

Stewart was insistent, and Blackmun finally agreed to say clearly that a fetus was not a person.

After he had joined Blackmun's opinion, Stewart still wanted to add his own concurrence. Unlike Douglas, he was not inclined to write separate opinions spelling out small, technical disagreements with the majority. Stewart often joined inadequate opinions—"junk," he once called them—believing that this was a vital part of the compromising process. It also left him more time to write his own majority opinions.

But the Blackmun opinion lacked an explicit constitutional foundation for the abortion ruling. In a middle section providing his legal reasoning, Blackmun had brought the broadest arguments against restrictive abortion laws. He had written a sweeping general conclusion that the basis for lifting the restrictions could be found in the Ninth and Fourteenth, even in the First Amendment, and that it was implied in a series of privacy cases, ranging from the 1965 Connecticut contraceptive case to the previous term's contraceptive case so carefully tailored by Brennan *(Eisenstadt v. Baird)*.

"Zones of privacy," Blackmun had written, do exist "under the Constitution." Stewart could not fully accept that. It was too broad. It was precisely the cause of his dissent in the 1965 Connecticut contraceptive case and of his hesitancy the previous year in *Eisenstadt.* He wanted to identify the part of the Constitution that conferred the freedom to have abortions during the early months of pregnancy. Stewart believed that a woman's right to an abortion in the early months was a "liberty" protected under the due process clause of the Fourteenth Amendment. But that approach carried with it historical baggage that Stewart would rather avoid.

In the 1930s the Court had used the clause to strike down key New Deal legislation. Since "liberty" could be construed to mean anything that five justices agreed should be protected, critics charged that the Court had become a superlegislature, substituting its judgment for that of elected legislators. This approach, called "substantive due process" (to differentiate it from the more common procedural rights covered by due process), had been gradually discredited.

Since Stewart felt that "substantive due process" was the real basis for the Blackmun opinion, he believed that Blackmun was hesitant to admit it in the opinion. Stewart circulated his own concurrence, joining Blackmun's opinion, but adding his observations on the real roots of the opinion.

Reading Stewart's concurrence, Douglas found it laughable that Stewart, of all people, was concerned with constitutional purity. Douglas believed that Stewart's real motive in writing a concurrence was to put some distance between himself and Blackmun's opinion, which Stewart obviously thought was poorly reasoned and written.

Douglas shot back a memo arguing that Stewart had the history all wrong. This was not "substantive due process," Douglas said. He had been one of the earliest and most vociferous critics of that doctrine. The basis for the decision was clear. The Blackmun opinion was based on the right to privacy, Douglas countered.

Blackmun wanted no part of the Stewart-Douglas debate. He was tired of compromising and dealing with everyone's gripes. This latest "sniping" was ridiculous. The important thing was that he already had six votes.

Given his gloomy expectations at the outset of the abortion debate, Douglas felt the Court had come a long way. The right to privacy was being given constitutional foundation in a major opinion. He dropped his debate with Stewart. It was a great victory, and Douglas wanted to add a concurring opinion underscoring its significance.

He decided to revise a lyrical concurrence that he had drafted the previous term about what he called the

> customary, traditional, and time-honored rights, amenities, privileges and immunities that come within the sweep of "the Blessings of Liberty."
>
> First is the autonomous control over the development and expression of one's intellect, interests, tastes and personality.

Second is freedom of choice in the basic decisions of one's life respecting marriage, divorce, procreation, contraception, and the education and upbringing of children.

Third is the freedom to care for one's health and person, freedom from bodily restraint or compulsion, freedom to walk, stroll, or loaf.

A clerk urged him to go beyond his discussion of a right to privacy and conclusively nail down a right to abortion.

Douglas responded, "I'm only writing this for me."

White shortened his dissent from the previous term. The states, not the courts, should decide the question of limits on abortion. Blackmun's trimester-and-viability scheme was pure legislation. "As an exercise of raw judicial power, the Court perhaps has authority to do what it does today," White wrote. But he expressed doubts about a constitutional sanction that would allow a woman to get rid of an unwanted child on a "whim" or out of "caprice."

"The Court," White wrote, "apparently values the convenience of the pregnant mother more than the continued existence and development of the life or potential life that she carries."

Rehnquist's dissent had little to do with abortion. As always, Rehnquist pushed his views on restricting federal court powers and the women's rights to bring these cases into court. First, he attacked the most basic element of the cases. No one had standing to bring these cases into court, he said. Assuming the women were pregnant when the suit was brought, they would be at least in their third trimester by the time the lower court decided the case. Since Blackmun's opinion held that states could deny abortions during the third trimester, there was no claim for the women to bring.

Rehnquist pointed out that in 1868, when the Fourteenth Amendment was adopted, at least 36 states or territories had laws on the books limiting abortions. It did not appear that the framers of the Fourteenth Amendment intended to bar the states from regulating abortions.

———

By early December, Blackmun's final draft had circulated. Stewart's and Douglas's concurrences were finished, and White's and Rehnquist's dissents were ready. There was still nothing from Burger.

White was particularly unhappy with the progress of the term. Dozens of cases were ready to come down except, more often than not, for the chief's vote. He wrote a memo pointing out the bottleneck.

By early January, there was still nothing from the chief. Blackmun grew increasingly nervous. He was worried about his reputation for being chronically late. He had not yet brought down an opinion for the term. Abortion was ready; he wanted it to come down at once. Blackmun and the others in the majority finally began pointing toward a Monday, January 15, 1973, announcement of the abortion decisions. Still there was nothing from Burger.

On January 12 at conference, Stewart put it to the chief directly. "Vote now or let the decision come down with only eight votes," Stewart suggested.

To the majority's surprise, Burger said that he had decided to join the Blackmun opinion but, like some of the others, he wanted to add his own concurring remarks. "I'll get it to you next week," he promised.

Stewart and Brennan thought he was stalling. The chief was scheduled to swear in Richard Nixon for his second term as president on January 20. It would undoubtedly be embarrassing for Burger to stand there, swearing in the man who had appointed him, having just supported a sweeping and politically volatile opinion that repudiated that man's views.

At the Friday, January 19, conference, the chief said that his schedule had been busy, and he still had not gotten to the abortion decision. Stewart figured that, having manipulated a delay until after the inaugural, Burger would acquiesce. The others wanted a Monday, January 22, announcement, three days later, and Burger said that he would have something.

Over the weekend, he wrote a three-paragraph concurrence. Ignoring the sweep of the opinion he was joining, Burger said that one law (Texas) was being struck because it did not permit abortions in instances of rape or incest, and he implied that the other law was being struck because of the "complex" steps that required hospital board certification of an abortion. He did not believe that the opinion would have the "consequences" predicted by dissenters White and Rehnquist, and he was sure that states could still control abortions. "Plainly," he concluded, "the Court today rejects any claim that the Constitution requires abortion on demand."

———

The day of the scheduled abortion decision the chief sat in his chambers reading the latest edition of *Time* magazine. "Last week TIME learned that the Supreme Court has decided to strike down nearly every anti-abortion law in the land," an article said. The abortion decision had been leaked.

Burger drafted an "Eyes Only" letter to the other justices. He wanted each justice to question his law clerks. The responsible person must be found and fired. Burger intended to call in the FBI to administer lie-detector tests if necessary.

Dutifully, Rehnquist brought up the matter with his clerks. It was harmless in this case, he said. But in a business case, a leak could affect the stock market and allow someone to make millions of dollars. None of Rehnquist's clerks knew anything about the leak, but they asked him if it were true that the chief was thinking of lie-detector tests. "It is still up in the air," Rehnquist said. "But yes, the chief is insisting."

Rehnquist's clerks were concerned. Such a witch-hunt would be met with resistance. Certainly, some clerks would refuse to take such a test and would probably have to resign. The chief is mercurial, Rehnquist explained. "The rest of us will prevail on him."

Brennan summoned his clerks and read them the chief's letter. It was another example, he said, of the chief usurping the authority each justice had over his own clerks. "No one will question my law clerks but me," Brennan said. Then in a softer voice, he added, "And I have no questions." The real outrage for Brennan was not the leak but the delay. If the chief had not been intent on saving himself and Nixon some embarrassment on Inauguration Day, there probably would have been no damaging leak.

Marshall asked what his clerks knew about the incident. When he was assured that they knew nothing, he told them to forget it.

Douglas treated the letter as he had treated a request from the chief the previous term that all clerks be instructed to wear coats in the hallways. He ignored it.

Powell was out of town, so one of his clerks opened the chief's letter. The clerk had talked to the *Time* reporter, David Beckwith, trying to give him some guidance so he could write an intelligent story when the decision came down. But the delay in announcing the decision had apparently left *Time* with a scoop, if only for half a day.

The clerk called Powell and told him about the chief's letter and his own terrible mistake in talking to Beckwith. He volunteered to resign.

That would not be necessary, Powell said. But a personal explanation would have to be given to the chief.

Powell called Burger and explained that one of his clerks, a brilliant and talented young lawyer, was responsible. The clerk realized his mistake and had learned his lesson. The clerk went to see the chief.

Burger was sympathetic. Reporters were dishonest and played tricks, he said. It was a lesson everyone had to learn.

Apparently never expecting to learn so much about the little deceptions of both reporters and sources, Burger pressed for all the details. It took nearly 45 minutes to satisfy his curiosity.

The clerk concluded that Burger understood, that he was being a saint about the matter. Burger wanted a memo detailing exactly what happened. The clerk would not have to resign.

Later, the chief met with top editors of *Time* in an off-the-record session. He labeled Beckwith's efforts to get inside information at the Court improper, the moral equivalent of wiretapping.

Blackmun suggested to his wife, Dottie, that she come to Court to hear case announcements on Monday, January 22. He did not tell her why. As Blackmun announced the decisions, Powell sent a note of encouragement to Blackmun's wife. Powell suspected they were about to witness a public outcry, the magnitude of which he and Blackmun had not seen in their short time on the Court.

"I'm very proud of the decision you made," Dottie later told her husband.

After the abortion decision was announced, Blackmun took congratulatory calls through most of the afternoon. But former president Lyndon Johnson died the same day, and the news of his death dominated the next morning's newspapers.

Blackmun was unhappy that the abortion decision did not get more attention. Many women, especially the poor and Black, would not learn of their new rights. But the outcry quickly began, led by the Catholic Church. "How many millions of children prior to their birth will never live to see the light of day because of the shocking action of the majority of the United States Supreme Court today?" demanded New York's Terence Cardinal Cooke.

John Joseph Cardinal Krol, of Philadelphia, the president of the National Conference of Catholic Bishops, said, "It is hard to think of any decision in the 200 years of our history which has had more disastrous implications for our stability as a civilized society."

Thousands of letters poured into the Court. The guards had to set up a special sorting area in the basement with a huge box for each justice.

The most mail came to Blackmun, the decision's author, and to Brennan, the Court's only Catholic. Some letters compared the justices to the butchers of Dachau, child killers, immoral beasts and Communists. A special ring of hell would be reserved for the justices. Whole classes from Catholic schools wrote to denounce the justices as murderers. "I really don't want to write this letter but my teacher made me," one child said.

Minnesota Lutherans zeroed in on Blackmun. New Jersey Catholics called for Brennan's excommunication. Southern Baptists and other groups sent over a thousand bitter letters to Hugo Black, who had died 16 months earlier. Some letters and calls were death threats.

Blackmun went through the mail piece by piece. The sisters of Saint Mary's hospital, the backbone of the Mayo Clinic, wrote outraged letters week after week. He was tormented. The medical community and even his friends at Mayo were divided. Blackmun encountered picketing for the first time in his life when he gave a speech in Iowa. He understood the position of the anti-abortion advocates, but he was deeply hurt by the personal attacks. He felt compelled to point out that there had been six other votes for the decision, besides his, that the justices had tried to enunciate a constitutional principle, not a moral one. Law and morality overlapped but were not congruent, he insisted. Moral training should come not from the Court but from the Church, the family, the schools.

The letters continued to pour in. Every time a clergyman mentioned the decision in his sermon, the letters trickled in for a month from members of the congregation. The attack gradually wore Blackmun down. At breakfast with his clerks, when the discussion turned to the decision, Blackmun picked up his water glass reflectively, turning it slightly on edge and staring into it in silence.

The criticism also drew Blackmun and Brennan closer. Blackmun wrote Brennan a warm thank-you note: "I know it is tough for you, and I thank you for the manner in which you made your suggestions."

Brennan tried to cheer up Blackmun. Doing the right thing

was not often easy, he said. The one thing in the world Brennan did not want known was his role in molding the opinion.*

Blackmun did not cheer up easily. The hysteria on each side of the issue convinced him that any decision would have been unpopular. However, the deepest cut came when the state of Texas filed a petition for rehearing that compared Blackmun's conclusion which held that a fetus was not a person, to the Court's infamous 1857 decision that said that Dred Scott, a slave, was not a citizen or person under the Constitution. Blackmun thought that comparing his opinion with the Court's darkest day of racism was terribly unfair. And, after all, it had been Stewart who had insisted on that part of the opinion.

Months later, Blackmun gave a speech at Emory Law School in Atlanta. He was chatting with students and faculty when a petite young woman with black curly hair ran up the steps to the stage. She squeezed through the group, threw her arms around Blackmun and burst into tears. "I'll never be able to thank you for what you have done. I'll say no more. Thank you."

The woman turned and ran from the room.

Blackmun was shaken. He suspected that the woman was probably someone who had been able to obtain an abortion after the Court's decision. He did not know that "Mary Doe," the pseudonym of the woman in Georgia who had filed one of the original abortion suits (*Doe v. Bolton*), had just embraced him.

---

* When the clerks later put together bound volumes of the opinions Brennan had written that term, they included the abortion opinions, and on page 156 they wrote, "These cases are included with Justice Brennan's opinions for the October term 1972 because the opinions for the Court were substantially revised in response to suggestions made by Justice Brennan."

CONCLUSION

THE RIGHT TO LIFE MOVEMENT HAD DEVELOPED tremendous momentum since Blackmun's 1973 abortion decision. Anti-abortion demonstrators gathered periodically at the Court, and some sent Blackmun roses on the anniversary of the decision. Blackmun, puzzled, nervous and grim, stood by his office window and watched the demonstrations. He felt that so much of the opposition reflected a misunderstanding of the Court's opinion and purpose.

Blackmun publicly defended the abortion decision, telling one audience that people "forget that the Court functions only on constitutional principles. All we were deciding was a constitutional issue, not a philosophical one. . . .

"A lot of people have personalized this, thinking it's the work of the devil, to wit, me—forgetting there were seven votes for that opinion."

Yet, Blackmun knew there was considerable unhappiness with the abortion decision within the Court. The original dissenters, Rehnquist and White, kept up a steady drumbeat. In one memo for the cert pool prepared by one of White's clerks, the doctor in an abortion case was called a "fetus killer." Blackmun was furious.

Rehnquist told college audiences that the Court might someday overturn the decision.

Since the 1973 decision, Burger had gone back to his original anti-abortion position, and Powell seemed shaky. While Douglas was on the Court, Blackmun was virtually certain in new abortion cases to have five solid votes to follow the 1973 decision. In 1975 after Douglas resigned because of ill health, President Gerald Ford nominated John Paul Stevens, a 55-year-old judge on the Seventh Circuit in Chicago, to become an associate justice of the Supreme Court. On December 10, he was confirmed by the full Senate 98 to 0. Douglas's resignation left the abortion issue in doubt. Blackmun did not believe that the decision would be overruled. But the 1973 decision had left some major questions open. Many states had enacted new laws that had the practical effect of restricting abortions.

A 1974 Missouri law put a number of limitations on abortions including requirements that:

- an unmarried woman under the age of 18 obtain her parents' consent before an abortion.

- a married woman obtain her husband's written consent.

- saline amniocentesis, the most common abortion method, not be used after 12 weeks of pregnancy.*

In the 1976 term, the Court had considered a case *(Planned Parenthood v. Danforth)* that challenged these provisions of the Missouri law. At first, Blackmun had insisted that the Court summarily—without oral argument—reverse the lower court

---

* The method involves inserting a needle into the womb and injecting a saline solution, which induces labor and a miscarriage.

opinion upholding the Missouri law. A summary reversal would be the fastest and most conclusive way to tell the lower court that its decision was wrong, and that prior decisions clearly predetermined the opposite result. Summary reversal was to tell the lower court that it had clearly misread a Supreme Court opinion. A summary opinion merely called the lower court's attention to the previous, controlling opinion.

Blackmun had written a 30-page per curiam summary reversal that said that the states could do little to regulate abortions. But when it circulated, Burger, Powell, Rehnquist and White refused to join. At the time, Douglas had not resigned yet but was ill and there was an informal agreement nullifying his vote when it was the fifth, Blackmun had only four votes. That meant the case would have to be heard during the 1975–76 term. But if the Court announced that it was going to hear oral argument, the anti-abortion forces would mobilize. Blackmun and Brennan, in particular, did not want to give those forces the summer to mount an attack. They devised a plan. The Court would not announce that it would hear the case until the beginning of the next term. The announcement that the case would be heard was made on October 6, 1975.

Later in the 1976 term, at conference on the case, Blackmun got five votes to strike each of the controversial provisions of the Missouri law.* Stewart was unhappy about going along with what

---

* Powell voted with Blackmun, Brennan, Marshall and Stewart to strike the requirement of parental consent and the ban on the saline abortion method. Rehnquist, White and Burger were in dissent on those issues and joined by Justice John Paul Stevens, Douglas's successor. But Stevens joined the liberals as a sixth vote on striking the provision requiring the husband's consent.

he felt were further analytical errors, but since he had voted for the original 1973 decision, he saw no alternative on this one. "This is one of those cases where I'll have to hold my nose and jump," he told his clerks.

The conference also considered another abortion case *(Singleton v. Wulff)* that raised the question of whether doctors had standing to bring suit challenging a Missouri state law that prevented poor women from obtaining federally funded abortions. The first vote at conference was 5 to 4 to grant doctors standing for such lawsuits. The majority was an unusual combination of Brennan, Marshall, White, Stevens and, to nearly everyone's surprise, Burger. But again to everyone's surprise, Blackmun voted to deny standing. He told others that he was bothered by law journal articles criticizing his 1973 decision for conferring more rights on doctors performing abortions than on women receiving them. Burger then decided to switch his vote, making it 5 to 4 to deny standing to doctors.

Stewart, who had voted to deny standing at first, said he now wanted to change his vote to grant standing. That made it 5 to 4 again in favor of standing.

At that point Burger said he was not sure of his position. However, he told Brennan, the senior member of the latest majority, to assign the opinion. Brennan also was to assign a third abortion case *(Bellotti v. Baird)* in 1979, which involved a remand to a lower court. It gave him three abortion cases, his most important assignment opportunity of the term. His clerks urged him to give all three cases to Marshall. Brennan balked. Important bridges had been built to Blackmun, and they were based more on the abortion issue than on any other. Blackmun would surely want the two cases in which he was in the majority. The problem remained that

Blackmun was in the minority on the third dealing with doctors' standing. Clearly he could not write the majority opinion on that one. Brennan telephoned Blackmun to explain that he would have wanted to give him all three abortion cases, but that his minority position on doctors' standing made it impossible.

"I can write it that way," Blackmun replied.

Brennan was startled, but he was not about to question Blackmun's decision to switch his vote. Without hesitation, Brennan assigned him all three cases, hoping that he would remain a solid vote in future abortion fights.

Blackmun took months before circulating his first drafts in the three cases. Brennan went through the drafts thoroughly and had his clerks list dozens of suggested changes. But, before he proposed them, he joined Blackmun's drafts.

White thought the Blackmun drafts were dreadful. Blackmun's 1973 abortion opinion had subjected the Court to a great deal of ridicule. It was as if Blackmun had developed a special constitutional rule for handling medical questions. White dubbed it Blackmun's "medical question doctrine." It seemed to hold that, under the Constitution, doctors, rather than the Court, had the final authority on certain medical-legal questions. White found that notion ludicrous. Blackmun had created another "political questions" doctrine. The notion that the Court couldn't meddle in the internal affairs of the other branches of government had been broadened to include the medical profession.

White was particularly incensed about the section of the Blackmun draft on saline abortions. Blackmun had written that there was no "evidence" that the method was unsafe. What Blackmun meant, White felt, was that he had found no "medical evidence," based on his own independent research of medical texts and journals. However, "evidence" *had* been introduced in the lower court showing that saline abortions were less safe than other methods of abortion. That, White felt, was the "evidence" on which the Supreme Court should make its decision.

Blackmun appeared to have appointed himself—and, in turn, the Court—an unofficial medical board. To White, it was ridiculous. The normal rules of law and procedure had been abandoned. The Court could not go around making determinations on medical "facts," and substituting those facts for the ones that had been properly developed in the trial court. White wrote a strong dissent.

For his part, Blackmun was edgy about the abortion cases. He dropped a load of books on a desk one day and blurted out: "Fetuses!" Though he finally got five votes for each major part of his opinions, only Brennan and Marshall joined him in all the cases.

ACKNOWLEDGMENTS

This book has two sponsors, Benjamin C. Bradlee, the executive editor of *The Washington Post*, and Richard Snyder, president of Simon and Schuster. Without their support and encouragement this book would have been impossible. No other newspaper editor or book publisher would have been as willing to assume the risks inherent in a detailed examination of an independent branch of government whose authority, traditions and protocols have put it beyond the reach of journalism.

At Simon and Schuster, we also owe special thanks to Sophie Sorkin, Frank Metz, Edward Schneider, Wayne Kirn, Gwen Edelman, Alberta Harbutt, Joni Evans, Harriet Ripinsky.

To Alice Mayhew, our editor, we give our respect and affection for her constant support and guidance as she nurtured this book to completion.

At *The Washington Post* we also thank Katharine Graham, Donald Graham, Howard Simons, the late Laurence Stern, Elizabeth Shelton, Julia Lee, Carol Leggett, Lucia New, Rita Buxbaum, Adam Dobrin.

A critical reading and numerous suggestions were provided by Karen De Young, Marc Lackritz, Ann Moore, Jim Moore, Bob Reich, Ronald Rotunda, Bob Wellen and Douglas Woodlock.

Tom Farber helped greatly with suggestions and writing.

Milt Benjamin, our colleague at the *Post*, devoted several months to recrafting, editing and rewriting the initial drafts. We will never be able to thank him enough.

We owe and give our greatest thanks to our sources.

Washington, D.C.
August 1979

INDEX

ABOUT THE AUTHORS

Bob Woodward is an associate editor at *The Washington Post* where he has worked for 50 years and reported on every American president from Nixon to Trump. He has shared in two Pulitzer Prizes, first for the *Post*'s coverage of the Watergate scandal with Carl Bernstein, and second 20 years later as the lead *Post* reporter for coverage of the 9/11 terrorist attacks.

Scott Armstrong is executive director of the Information Trust. A former reporter for *The Washington Post*, he founded the National Security Archive and was a senior investigator for the Senate Watergate Committee.